# Redirecting Children's Behavior

# Redirecting Children's Behavior

**4TH EDITION**

*Effective Discipline for Creating Connection and Cooperation*

## KATHRYN J. KVOLS

CHICAGO

Fourth edition
Published by Parenting Press
An imprint of Chicago Review Press Incorporated
814 North Franklin Street
Chicago, Illinois 60610
ISBN 978-1-64160-761-2


Library of Congress Control Number: 2022933858


Cover design: Jonathan Hahn
Cover photographs: istock.com/LumiNola
Typesetting: Nord Compo

Printed in the United States of America
5 4 3 2 1

For our children and their children

*Lord, make me an instrument of thy peace.*
—Saint Francis of Assisi

# Contents

# Foreword

**What we know and believe** about children and families has changed dramatically in the last twenty-five years. Parents, teachers, and coaches recall the "good old days" when you could tell kids to do something and they jumped and did it. Kids today, on the other hand, are requesting respect and democracy, especially in the autocracies that control their homes, classrooms, and athletic fields. The result is confusion and power struggles with parents and professionals, and often, we don't know why we're struggling.

If you step back and look at the progress we've made in understanding children, it's astonishing how far we've come in the last quarter of a century. It was not until the late 1960s and early 1970s, through the work of Dr. T. Berry Brazelton and others, that we became aware that infants could see, hear, feel, and actively contribute to their relationships with their parents. How magnificent! With this finding, we began to view children, even at the beginning of their lives, as participants in the family process. Children have become powerful, emphatic collaborators to be respected rather than clay for us to mold and control. It's no wonder that many of us have experienced confusion and chaos.

So here is Kathryn Kvols's book, *Redirecting Children's Behavior*, offering us the tools we need to develop the closeness with our children and families that we want so very much. Kathryn believes, as I do, that every person is born whole, perfect, and connected to everyone and everything. Through experiences as children, with parents, siblings, and others, we are socialized and wounded in ways that cause us to lose our awareness of the connections with others. This book offers us the means to reconnect. It provides the framework and process for parenting so that we learn to relate to children in a way that supports their development, creating adults who feel whole and free and able to experience closeness and intimacy with others.

—Timothy J. Jordan, MD

# Introduction

There is no love in hurry.
—Mother Theresa

**I**t was early. I hadn't finished packing yet for a keynote presentation to a group of some four hundred participants. I was hurrying everyone around me. I needed to drop off my nine-year-old son, Tyler, at school before I went to the airport. In the car, a heated argument started between the two of us. It ended with Tyler angrily getting out of the car, me throwing his backpack at his feet, and Tyler slamming the door.

The pain of having such a disturbing argument and leaving it without resolution was excruciating for me. Tears were streaming down my face along with my makeup. Rushed onstage, there I was in front of a packed audience eagerly waiting. They had all paid good money to hear my parenting words of wisdom. I stood there frozen, unable to speak. The speech that I had been preparing for weeks was completely wiped from my memory. I tried helplessly to fight back my tears, but my eyes continued to well up. After I explained to my audience what had happened, there was not a dry eye in the audience. Everyone could relate and I could feel a collective sigh of relief that parenting was not about perfection.

This book is not about striving for perfection. It is about taking baby steps and letting those baby steps be the milestone to becoming your best parenting version.

Children touch the very depths of our souls. One moment we're feeling love and joy; the next moment, frustration and incompetence, and, at times, despair. Children test you and make you examine the very core of your belief systems. But if you are willing to investigate these belief systems, you can be the catalyst for transformation in your family.

Many new and exciting things have been added since the last edition of this book, including:

- How to establish and maintain a growth mindset
- Tips to help you and your child manage emotions effectively
- Steps to set clear limits and follow through
- How to move beyond using consequences to implement change
- New ways to enhance the parent-child connection through even the most difficult altercations
- And much more

This book is based on a culmination of more than thirty years of experience teaching parenting courses. It is filled with real-life examples gleaned from thousands of parents and professionals using these principles throughout the world. The tools are easy, practical, and can be implemented immediately.

Parents have said *Redirecting Children's Behavior* is not just a form of discipline but a way of life. When family members sense that you aren't trying to coerce them, they become respectful and self-reliant. Richer conversations are had, and this increases the level of cooperation and fun you experience. Life becomes more meaningful.

The family unit is the fabric of which our countries are woven. As we lean into love, we experience more heartfelt connections within families, with friends, and with coworkers. As a result, societies will become more collaborative, and isolation and violence will be diminished.

I am honored to be here on this parenting journey with you. It is a walk like none other.

—Kathryn J. Kvols

# 1

# Inside-Out Parenting

*Self-care is giving the world the best of you, not what's left of you.*
—KATIE REED

**Your son has just** spilled his juice on the carpet. It's no big deal, but you really lose your temper this time. Why do you react so strongly now and not the last time he spilled juice? One reason we parents become irritable, overwhelmed, depressed, or sick is that we have not been doing a very good job of taking care of ourselves. How long has it been since you had thirty minutes by yourself to do whatever you wanted? Common answers I hear are "I can't remember," or "I don't have time to do that."

Just before the airplane takes off, the flight attendant instructs parents to place the oxygen mask on themselves first in an emergency, and then place a mask on their child. Notice the request: put yours on first, then you will be able to help your child. All too often we satisfy the needs of our children and other people before our own. As a result, our energy is depleted and we have nothing left to give, or we give with resentment. Even a minor problem challenges our used-up reserves.

Why don't parents take care of themselves? Some reasons are:
- We've been taught that it's selfish to take care of ourselves.
- We feel that taking quiet time or "downtime" is not good use of our time.

- We don't believe that we deserve time for ourselves.
- We believe that we just don't have, or can't find, the time.
- We don't know how to take care of ourselves.

What do you look like and sound like when you haven't taken time for yourself? I know I am grouchy, not fun, impatient, and critical. Burned out is a good description. This is the part of you your family experiences.

What do you look like and sound like when you do take care of yourself? There is much to gain when we take good care of ourselves. We are:

- Refreshed and have more energy for our children
- More confident and creative when our children spring surprises on us
- Ready and eager to spend time with our families
- Teaching our children, by example, how to take care of themselves

## Nurture Yourself

It is crucial for every parent to have at least thirty minutes each day to restore energy. Finding time for yourself takes commitment, creativity, and determination. The opportunities are not always obvious. Here are some of my ideas for time alone; add your own and take time for renewal.

- Get up earlier or go to bed later than everyone else in your household.
- Use your lunch hour for time alone—walking, thinking, reading, meditating, or dreaming.
- Hire a babysitter, or swap babysitting with a relative or friend, for a couple of hours.
- Alternate time off with your partner, so that you both benefit.

In addition to scheduling time alone, parents need to do things that give them pleasure and nurture them, just as they do this for their children. Do things for yourself that make you feel better. The following ideas might get you started; add your own to the list.

- Take bubble baths or long, hot showers that relax you. Music and candlelight can be delightful additions to the experience and raise it above the ordinary.
- Take walks, especially in the rain or snow.
- Get a professional massage.
- Listen to relaxing music or motivational CDs or podcasts.
- Meditate.
- Sit or work in the garden or in a local park.
- Write in your journal, putting down both the pleasant and unpleasant events of the day.
- Create something: draw, paint, or build.
- Play a musical instrument.

A mother of three children under the age of five told me how impossible it was for her to get away alone. I told her I understood; however, I wanted her to commit to finding some way to take care of herself. When she came back to class the following week, she looked great. Everyone wanted to know what she had done.

She told us, "I used to love playing the piano, but I haven't played it since the kids were born. The day it rained last week, things were really getting out of control. I just wanted to scream. Then I remembered my commitment and sat down at the piano. It was amazing! I worked out all my frustrations! I noticed that the kids had gathered around behind me and got calmer too."

The most important thing that I can tell you is to take care of yourself. If you take time for yourself, you will be ready for the constant demands that parenting places on you. Everything you are about to learn from this book will feel easier and come more naturally because you will have the energy to make changes.

## Eliminate Stress

Another way to take care of yourself is to work on eliminating as much stress as you can in your life. Let's look at your day. What segment of your day is the most stressful? Is it your morning routine, picking up the kids from school, homework time, the hour before dinner or bedtime? Take steps to counteract the toll it takes on you and your family. Here are some parents' solutions:

> A father found it extremely stressful to go directly from work to home with its flood of three children, all under the age of six, eagerly greeting him. So he made an agreement with his family that he would listen to some soothing music before he came home. Frequently he had to drive around the block a couple of times. By the time he got home, he was more relaxed and in a better frame of mind to be with his wife and children.

> A mother decided that the morning was her most stressful time. Getting her three-year-old daughter dressed became a huge battle that often made her late to work. To solve her problem, the mom gave her daughter a bath and dressed her in her clothes for preschool the night before. Her mornings became hassle free!

> A mother of a five-year-old realized she was most stressed when running errands immediately after picking up her daughter from preschool. The time was pure torture because her daughter would whine and fuss, refuse to get out of the car, and then refuse to get back in the car to go. The mother decided to take her daughter to a park and play with her for fifteen minutes before running her errands. After doing this for a week, she reported that her daughter had become more cooperative once she got some quality connection time with her mom.

## Self-Reflection Leads to Self-Growth

Learning about self-care also requires self-reflection. The reason this chapter is called "Inside-Out Parenting" is that being an effective parent requires that we become introspective. This involves reflecting on why we do or don't do certain things. What is going on in your family is often a reflection of what is going on in your inner self.

Self-reflection can be a scary and humbling experience. You may have an impulse to avoid it, but it is necessary for your growth. Self-reflection leads to self-improvement. Without introspection, we go blindly on our parenting path, creating unintended consequences. We fail to achieve our wishes and hopes for creating the picture we have of what it means to be a healthy family.

It is crucial that when you do self-reflection you do so with self-acceptance—looking at yourself neutrally, with curiosity. When introspection includes feelings of guilt, blame, or shame, we literally slow down the process of self-growth. These feelings make us want to hide and not take the risks necessary to create the connection and intimacy we all long for.

## Happiness Thieves

Do you engage in worry, guilt, anger, resentment, shame, blame, and overwhelm? These feelings all zap your energy, steal your joy, and keep you from being fully present with your children. It is your choice whether you let these feelings in to steal your happiness.

Let's look at them individually.

### Worry

Worry is a misuse of the mind. You know all too well that we spend a disproportionate amount of time worrying about things that are fundamentally outside of our control. You can worry yourself sick because there is an inordinate number of things you can worry about as a parent. The "what-ifs" can feel exhausting. You know the "What if she fails at school? What if he hangs out with the wrong kids? What if he decides not to go to college?" Worry never changes anything; it just messes with your mind.

> One mom caught herself spinning out of control with worry often, so she turned some spiritual music up loud, danced, and sang around the house. She found that her children often joined her!

Don't waste energy worrying about a problem; instead, trust that life will work out.

> When my son, Tyler, was five years old, we were driving up a winding road through a large piece of property my husband and I had just purchased for our business. The property was run down and in need of extensive repair before our opening day. My son looked at me and said, "Mommy, what's that face?" This was the question he always asked when I appeared to be discouraged.
> "I guess I'm worried," I said.
> "Worried? About what?" he asked.
> I answered, "I'm worried about money."
> Tyler replied reprovingly, "Mommy, don't you know life works?"

If you find yourself worrying, remind yourself that "life works." Take one small action to improve on the situation and let go. Worrying is literally betting against your ability to handle what life throws at you and betting against your trust in the divine.

## Guilt

Guilt is something that happened in the past that you let keep you from being present. If you allow it, guilt erodes your self-esteem and takes you away from the present moment because you are obsessing about the past.

If you are feeling guilty about something, the first step is to ask yourself, "What have I learned?" or "What will I do differently?"

The next step is to ask yourself if you need to forgive yourself or if you need to make amends to someone, or both.

If you need to forgive yourself, do so quickly. Otherwise, your guilt can compromise your ability to parent effectively. For example:

> After I got divorced from my husband, I felt guilty about not doing everything in my power to make the marriage work. I erroneously felt like I was robbing my son of the experience of having an intact family. As a result, I found myself compromising my values by doing

something I now call "guilt parenting." I would allow my son to stay up later than he should, give in to his tantrums, and feel sorry for my son.

As a result, my son was starting to act entitled, and I began to realize the toll my guilt was having on both of us. So I began the process of forgiving myself. Some people are able to forgive themselves quickly. For me, it was a process.

Becoming stronger in my convictions built my confidence. I no longer debilitated my son by feeling sorry for him, nor did I give in to his tantrums. I set clear limits and followed through.

What if guilt was designed to give you an opportunity to get back into integrity with yourself and/or others? If you feel you have harmed someone physically or emotionally it is important that you get back into integrity by making amends. Making amends not only makes you feel integrous but also restores the trust in your relationship.

> *There is one thing that is common to every individual, organization, nation, and civilization throughout the world. One thing which, if removed, will destroy the most powerful government, the most successful business, the most thriving economy, the most influential leadership, the greatest friendship, and the deepest love.*
>
> *On the other hand, if developed and leveraged, that one thing has the potential to create unparalleled success and prosperity in every dimension of life. Yet, it is the least understood, most neglected, and most underestimated possibility of our time.*
>
> *What is it?*
>
> *That one thing is trust.*
>
> —STEPHEN COVEY WITH REBECCA MERRILL, *THE SPEED OF TRUST*

In our family, we do make ups. If someone has made an error, we make our best effort not impose guilt or shame on one another and instead offer that person the opportunity to do a make up.

For example, early in our marriage my husband would frequently come home late from work. I would get pissy and the evening usually fell silent—a deadening silent. We decided to stop this nonsense by doing a make up. I feel transported when someone rubs my feet. So, on the nights he came home late, I got an amazing foot rub. I had no need to get even, and my husband could feel back in integrity in our relationship. This outcome was a lot more fun than giving my husband the silent treatment.

Children can write notes of apology, draw pictures, do chores for each other, or give back rubs. The ideas here are endless. No need to get even when you keep things even!

## *Anger*

Have you noticed how a small child gets angry, lets off steam, and then goes on his or her merry way? Some of us learned to stuff our anger inside instead. Unacknowledged anger can lead to depression, illness, and resentment. It can surface later as retaliation toward others. When we have learned to stuff anger, we often respond inappropriately to events and issues in our lives. Use these six steps to help you manage your anger positively.

## Anger Management

**1. Watch for the early warning signs of anger.** You may get tense somewhere in your body, such as your jaw or stomach, or your hands may start to perspire. These physical signs tell you that you need to take appropriate action.

**2. Acknowledge and explore your anger.** It doesn't help to stuff or deny your anger. Say to yourself, "I feel angry. What am I feeling angry about? Is this really about what my kid just did or didn't do? Or am I really angry about something else, such as my job, spouse, the stress I allow in my life, or something else?"

**3. Take a break to cool off.** Count to ten, go to your room, take a walk, or otherwise remove yourself emotionally or physically from the situation.

**4. After you have cooled off, take action.** When you take action, you feel less like a victim and more like a person in control of your life.

**5. Tell the person what you're angry about** (might not be possible in some cases): "I'm angry because the kitchen is a mess." Unlikely as it sounds, a simple statement of the problem can help solve it. Start with an "I" statement rather than a "you" statement: attack the problem, not the person. Notice that there is no name-calling, blame, or exaggeration in your simple statement of fact.

**6. Speak up clearly, quickly, and lovingly.** Our family members are not mind readers. Make a clear and concise statement about what you want. "I will make dinner as soon as the kitchen is clean." If we don't speak up about what we want, it can turn into a grievance.

*Grievances bring turmoil while communication brings peace.*
—WAYNE DYER

One of the things that disturbs relationships the most is an unwillingness to have difficult conversations. Communicating our grievances can feel difficult. We would rather get our tooth pulled than have one of those conversations. Fear of rejection, losing control, and saying things we regret all keep us from having authentic communication. However, talking is a way of releasing the energy that has built up and creates all the turmoil.

I have found talking about things as soon as I can rather than letting things fester and build up leads to better outcomes. So whether the conversation is with your child, your partner, your coworker, or one of your parents, have the conversation. Become an expert at speaking up clearly, quickly, and lovingly so that you can feel connected.

## Resentment

Unresolved anger can turn into resentment. Here is the definition of resentment: bitter indignation at having been treated unfairly.

People feel resentful in the following situations:
- They have given up something they want.
- They feel put down or disrespected.
- They are in relationship with someone who needs to be right or in control.
- They have been hurt or treated unfairly.
- They do more than their share of the work.

Frequently resentful people become so absorbed in their "injury" that they cannot stop thinking about the event(s) that caused their pain. Recurring negative and/or revengeful thoughts may take over and last for hours, days, and sometimes years. Self-blame occurs when the resentment and negative thoughts are turned inward. Regardless of the direction of the resentment—inward or outward—it can spill onto others, like our children.

Here are some questions to reflect on:
- What does my resentment cost me emotionally?
- Where do I need to learn to stick up for myself?
- How can I elicit more help?
- What things do I need to start saying no to?
- Is there someone I need to forgive?
- Is there someone in my life who is toxic, and do I need to minimize or eliminate my time spent with him or her?
- Whom do I need to forgive?

*The path to healing involves forgiveness and finding a way to make peace with what happened so you can move on with life.*

—UNKNOWN

## *Shame*

Shame is another one of those soul-eating emotions. When we experience shame, we feel disconnected, not good enough, and unworthy of receiving love. Thus, we are more likely to get depressed and engage in self-destructive behaviors like addiction. We try to hide that part of us as though it were something dirty and offensive. We may use shame to manipulate others.

> *If we can share our story with someone who responds with empathy and understanding, shame can't survive.*
> —BRENÉ BROWN

Understand that to be human is to have some skeletons in our closets. You would have to be a saint not to.

In a personal growth class I taught, we would have the participants write on a sheet of paper something they were ashamed of. Then we put the anonymous slips of paper in a pile in the middle of our circle. Everyone was instructed to pick up a sheet of paper and read what was written on that paper out loud as if they were the ones who had done the shameful deed. The results were astounding as everyone received the gift of relief that we all have done things we are not proud of, that we aren't some freak of nature undeserving of love.

If you decide to reveal your shame, make sure it is with someone you trust, someone who will have compassion and not judge you. I encourage you to find a therapist if you don't have someone in your life like this currently.

No longer feeling incapable of receiving love and needing to hide is a freeing feeling.

## *Blame*

I like to think of this work as "no fault" parenting. It is not the teacher's fault, not your parents' fault, not your child's fault, not your partner's fault, and not your fault.

Assigning blame to someone serves no good purpose and will generally wreak havoc on any relationship.

> *All blame is a waste of time. No matter how much fault you find with another, and regardless of how you blame him, it will not change you. The only thing blame does is to keep the focus off you when you are looking for external reasons to explain your unhappiness or frustration. You may succeed in making another feel guilty about something by blaming him, you won't succeed in changing whatever it is about you that is making you unhappy.*
> —WAYNE DYER

If you catch yourself blaming someone, refocus your energy on concentrating on what you can do to improve the situation. As much as I have tried, I have found that you can't change anyone but yourself.

## Overwhelm

A major cause of stress and anxiety for many people these days is overwhelm. In today's whirlwind world, we have access to so much information at the touch of a button. We are bombarded with advertising, which makes decision-making difficult. We find it nearly impossible to get away from texts, e-mails, or social media notifications.

Overwhelm can paralyze you and make you feel like a victim of your circumstances. Your mind gets cluttered, so it becomes difficult to think clearly. Overwhelm keeps you out of the present moment. As a result, it is hard to be creative and spontaneous, two ingredients useful for being a parent. Here are some effective ways to overcome overwhelm:

• **Brain dump:** Get it all on paper. In this way you have a clearer perspective of everything you "think" you have to do now.

• **Prioritize your list using the 4Ds method: delete, delay, delegate, or do.** Ask yourself, "Is this really important to get done? Does it need to be done today? Is there anyone else I can delegate this to?"

- **Lower your expectations:** Make your priority list and then aim to get only the three most important things done. Tell yourself that you will be satisfied when they are done. Move the rest of your list to tomorrow.
- **Change your emotional state:** To regain that open, creative, and confident mind, get your body moving! Physical exercise will change your state. Some jumping jacks, push-ups, or yoga poses can help. Going for a quick walk or a run can do the trick. For more fun, turn up the music and dance unabashedly around your house!
- **Set clear boundaries:** Learn to say no more often. Put a time limit on how long you will converse with your talkative friend. Limit the amount of extracurricular activities your kids can do. Setting boundaries may make you more unpopular in the short term but will keep you from feeling deluged in the long run.
- **Laugh at yourself:** Say something like this to yourself: "I ain't no victim! Who's in charge here anyway!" This helps you get life back into perspective.

In summary, these happiness thieves are the result of sloppy thinking. Challenge those thoughts by asking yourself, "Is this thought true? Is it helpful?" If it is neither of those, let them go and choose some more fun, life-giving thoughts.

All your power is in the present moment—not the past or the future. Become the bastion of your thoughts. Your sanity and health depend on it.

## Mistaken Beliefs

Self-care requires that we examine our mistaken beliefs. Most parents hold beliefs that interfere with their ability to be effective. One of them is a concern that our children always like us. This makes it difficult to set appropriate limits and be firm. We tend to give in to kids' pressures: "Well, all right, I'll buy you the toy if you stop crying."

Another mistaken belief is the desire to be indispensable. This interferes with our desire to raise self-reliant children. At first, we are truly indispensable. Without us, our children would not survive. However, when our children are older, we often do too much for them, either out of desire to have a role in their lives, to be valuable, or to avoid the more difficult challenges that confront us as adults. It is easier for us to succeed in the tasks of tying shoes and getting children started on time in the morning than it is to work on our own dreams.

As we turn more responsibilities over to our children, it's easy to feel as if we are no longer valuable or have a purpose. However, our task as parents is to work ourselves out of that job. We must allow our children to experience the successes and failures that teach them self-confidence and self-reliance as they grow.

The mistaken belief that you must be in control will cause problems when your children threaten or challenge your need for control (as they inevitably will if this is your belief). Whenever you try to make your children do something, you're very likely to have a power struggle on your hands.

At other times parents may find, upon self-reflection, that their children's behavior is bringing up unresolved issues from their own childhoods. I recall that when my son started normal exploration of his sexuality, I was concerned and upset. What I discovered was that his exploration brought back painful memories of my childhood. I was painfully shamed by my parents for my normal sexual curiosity. Consequently, I overreacted to Tyler's normal, healthy exploration.

These situations are especially likely to provoke overreaction: children fighting, anyone being angry or crying, poor grades, unfinished chores, money concerns, and eating issues. When you overreact in any of these situations, look back to your childhood and think about how your parents dealt with them.

What did you decide then that may be getting in the way now? For example, if you weren't allowed to express anger as a child, you might not want your child to be angry. Or if you were forced to eat certain food, you might try to force your child or be too lenient with food issues. After reflection ask yourself, "What do I want my children to learn from the situation that will be healthier for them?"

My children were my barometer I used to measure my inner peace. Usually, they misbehaved when I was not at peace. I checked in with myself (self-reflection) to see what was amiss. Sometimes I found I had been working too hard, hadn't taken time for myself, hadn't spent enough time with my family, or had some unresolved issues popping up.

## How to Handle Challenges Wisely

### *Refuse to be Offended*

Have you ever noticed that a huge percentage of conversations among adults are about what they are offended by? They are offended by the weather, their kids, their partners, politics, their colleagues, and on and on. Being offended is irksome and is a false way to connect with others by joining in their misery. This one is a tough one.

> Just last week I was on a lovely one-on-one vacation with my daughter. We were in an expensive hotel. I needed a shower. As I jumped in, I noticed a used washcloth in the nook of the shower. Neither one of us had taken a shower yet so I knew housekeeping had left it there unnoticed. Boy did I get offended. I thought, "I spent good money on this hotel, and it is not even clean." I must have gone off on thoughts like these for several minutes. I picked up the phone to call management to complain when I started cracking up with laughter. I realized that I was letting this little washcloth disturb my peace and interfere with these precious moments I had with my now-grown daughter.

Stop talking about what you are offended by and watch your happiness quotient soar.

Happiness is an inside job. Thinking things, people, and places will bring you happiness is erroneous thinking. They may give you temporary pleasure, but long-term happiness is generated from inside. It is a decision you make moment by moment.

Make your happiness and peace a priority. It is hard to live a joyful life when your cup is almost empty. Take responsibility for filling up that cup and demand less of others to fill it for you. Taking responsibility for your own happiness will also keep you from self-destructive behavior, such as drug addiction, overeating, complaining, alcoholism, smoking, insufficient exercise, and illness.

## Use Calming Self-Talk

Another way to handle challenges is to identify and manage your self-talk. Get rid of that voice in your head that expresses discouraging thoughts like "You are not good enough," "That was stupid," or "You can't get anything right." I do this by repeating a mantra as many times as necessary. My mantra is "I choose peace instead of this." Or you might want to try saying, "I am unlimited in power, peace, and love." In time, I find that I have chased away most of my negative thoughts and replaced them with more life-giving ones.

Elephants on parade in India would pull down tent poles and do other mischievous things with their trunks as they marched along. Their trainers discovered that if they gave the elephants short poles to carry, the animals were less disruptive. Like the elephant's pole, the repetitive, encouraging phrase can keep your mind from wandering into mischief.

## Let Go

Learning to let go is another way to deal with challenge. To do this, give a situation your best effort and then let go of the result. You can't control the result, and the more detached you are from it, the more peaceful you will be. Letting go means you trust your own or your child's innate wisdom, even when there is no visible evidence of it!

Let go when you are angry, worried, or feeling guilty or resentful; when you are trying to force someone to do something he or she doesn't want to do; and when you are tempted to nag, remind, or rescue inappropriately.

The best way to let go is to do something to calm down and relax. Remove yourself from the situation so that you can reflect on it from a distance. Take a walk or a soothing bath. Meditate. Read a book that inspires you. From the shelter of a calm outlook, we can usually find a peaceful way to handle a situation.

Many people think letting go is weak. However, letting go is a greater power than trying to control, defend, or hold on to your position.

Some people confuse indifference or not caring with letting go. For example, after several verbal bouts with your teenager, out of sheer frustration, you say in a resigned tone, "Oh, go to the party then. I don't care." This is not letting go! When you let go, you care deeply what the outcome will be. You simply know you have done your best and you have decided to trust that things will work out.

> My son was having a hard time learning to tell time. I decided to help him. I created one learning tool after another. I coached and coaxed until we were both exhausted. Nothing I did worked. Finally, I decided to let go. I comforted myself with the thought that surely by the time he was thirty years old, he would be able to tell time.
>
> A few months later my son asked for a watch for his birthday. The parenting gods smiled on me, and I refrained from saying, "Why? You can't read it." Instead, I bought the watch. Later in the week, I was due to pick up my son at 3:15 PM. I arrived at 3:17 PM and was greeted with, "You're late!"

### Ask Yourself, "What Am I Tolerating?"

Tolerating unwanted situations leads to frustration and ultimately anger and resentment. Chores not getting done, mess, lack of partner time, and back talk are just a few of the things we tolerate. When we put up with situations, we are likely to deal with them in unhealthy ways, such as the use of sarcasm, complaining, getting even, and other forms of passive-aggressive behavior. It is your job to keep things even so that you don't have to get even! Make it a goal of yours to reflect weekly on things you might be tolerating and make an effort to change things by using some of the techniques discussed in this book.

## What Do You Want?

One way I take care of myself is to determine what I want to have happen and then to make it happen. This leads to an increase in self-confidence. There was a time when I couldn't figure out what I wanted because I was too concerned about being liked. If my husband asked what movie I wanted to see, I'd respond by asking him what he wanted to see. With my children and in other relationships, I now ask myself, "What do I want to see happen in this situation?"

For example, if my child asks to go to the movies on a Sunday afternoon, I ask myself, "What do I want?" Do I want family time, or do I need time by myself or time alone with my husband? Once I know, then I negotiate accordingly with my husband or child.

## Life Is a Balancing Act

When life throws you a challenge it is much easier to deal with it effectively if you feel balanced in your life. Pay attention to these seven areas and keep them in balance so you feel alive and satisfied. If you aren't successful or fulfilled in one area, it may have an adverse effect on other areas. These areas are:

- Spiritual
- Physical
- Education; learning
- Financial
- Career; vocation
- Recreation; relaxation
- Social (family and friends, etc.)

Make a commitment to improve the balance where necessary. For example, if you don't exercise (a common problem for many of us), commit to finding a form of exercise that is enjoyable for you. If your finances are in disarray, take a class in budgeting.

Challenges will happen. The best way to deal with them is by making sure you are taking care of yourself. Here's your assignment: wake up every morning and plan how you will find time to take care of yourself.

# 2

# Ways to Empower Your Child

**I**f you were to ask a group of kindergartners, "How many of you believe you could be a great doctor, scientist, or president of the United States?" most hands would go up quickly and self-assuredly. When children are little, they are full of confidence; they believe they can do anything; they have unlimited potential. But ask that question of a group of teenagers and fewer than half will raise their hands. By the time we are adults, most of us have long since forgotten or given up our dreams. What happened?

Imagine your child's spirit as a brightly glowing flame that dances and grows with each piece of fuel you feed it. Now, imagine someone pouring sand on the flame. The result? Depending on how much sand and the speed at which it is poured, the flame fades or goes out.

We dampen or put out a child's flame (spirit) by nagging, yelling, spanking, being overprotective or controlling, and using threats, guilt, shame, or punishment to correct misbehavior.

Every day you have hundreds of opportunities to kindle a child's spirit, rather than dampen it. Encouragement is the way to keep your child's spirit burning brightly. Let's talk about the most important ways to do this.

## Honor Your Child's Unique Self

Parents tend to spend a great deal more time trying to mold their children to be different from who they are than honoring them as they are. Everywhere I go I hear phrases such as these:

- Don't be silly.
- Be quiet.
- Stop crying.
- Shame on you.
- You're so noisy.
- You're bad.
- Don't be sad.
- You're being selfish.
- You're just like . . .
- Why can't you be like . . .

There are many unhappy adults who are still doing (or not doing) something because of their parents' influence through small criticisms that leave lasting impressions. Respect and honor your child's uniqueness. Parents and children live best together when each can fully express who they are.

## Give Unconditional Love

Children need unconditional love from their parents. There is no greater gift for a child. This love doesn't depend on performance. It is given simply because a child *is*. There is nothing he or she must do, no paradigm or mold to fit into, no parental dream to live up to, no good grades or clean room required, to earn unconditional love. How many adults do you know who strive for love through "doing" and piling up accomplishments? These individuals probably did not experience unconditional love as children.

A client of mine told me how his parents' form of discipline was to withdraw their love from him when he did something they didn't approve of. He said their silent treatment was unbearable and he often felt worthless and alone.

I once saw an Instagram post that depicted the family life of a group of monkeys. When a baby monkey ran off and got into danger, the mother would get her baby and put it under her arm. Then she would lovingly stroke its head. I wish I could have shown this video to a woman I once saw at the airport. We were sitting and waiting to board the plane. This cute little redhead kept running out of his mom's sight. Mom kept barking, "Get back here. I can't see you!" Of course, he obeyed for a few seconds, and then took off as if taunting his mother. This scenario went on for at least thirty minutes with Mom making commands that then led to threats. I could feel the tension mounting. Luckily, the situation was defused when they had to board the plane.

Mom could have simply had her son come sit by her, connect for a few minutes, then say, "Are you ready to try again?" She may have had to use this method several times, but soon her youngster would have gotten the message.

Understand that every misbehavior is either an act of love or a cry for love and connection. Are you a loving person? Of course you are! Are you committed to expanding your ability to give your children the guidance they need and the unconditional love they deserve?

Unconditional love is essential in raising self-confident children who love themselves, others, and the world in which they live. It is only when we give our children this type of love that they are free to be the best version of themselves. Choose to lean into love.

## Believe in Your Child

An important aspect of unconditional love is belief in your child. Encouraging words and actions flow from this faith when you have a positive outlook. Our beliefs about our children shape how we respond to them. Sometimes we're not aware of our beliefs. To find out if your beliefs about your children are positive or negative, look at the labels you apply (sometimes unconsciously) to them. Sadly, for children, labels are more often negative than positive. Here are a few I often hear. Add your own to the list:

- Stupid
- Hyper
- Terrible two
- Teenager
- Lazy
- Forgetful
- Shy
- Brat

Labels put children in boxes that are hard to climb out of because they limit potential. Sometimes labels are excuses. They can give permission to continue unproductive behavior. At other times, they might seem positive ("pretty" or "genius"), but still limit a child because of our mental associations with the terms. And what happens to children for whom "pretty" is sufficient or "genius" makes them feel separate and alone?

If you have just realized you are limiting your child with labels, open your mind. Look for ways your "lazy" son is calm and unhurried. Help your "pretty princess" to feel capable and intelligent. Change the label and your expectations. Your child will respond positively.

## Support Your Child's Dreams

Discover what your children's dreams and aspirations are, and support them in fulfilling them. Children who are encouraged to explore and develop their passions are less likely to get into trouble. Remember that they are different from you and your belief in them has great influence on how they see themselves.

Do you ever expect and/or wish your child would fulfill your dreams? I know I did. I wanted to be a dancer. So I signed Brianna up for dancing lessons. This is a terrible burden for a child: she is put in the precarious position of wanting to please you and wanting to fulfill her own dreams. When the two desires are incompatible, the scene is set for disappointment and strife between you.

When you help children fulfill their dreams, you teach them they can accomplish what is important to them. This faith helps them maintain a healthy attitude about life. Adults who have given up their dreams often lead passionless and purposeless lives.

This father failed to honor his son's unique spirit, natural ability, and dream for himself:

> Dad wanted his son to be a dentist, a profession that provided a secure living. The son wanted to be a musician. After a lot of coercion, the son reluctantly went to dental school. The other students loved him because he would put dental terminology to music and play it on the piano to help everyone memorize before exams. After he completed his degree, he gave his diploma to his father and left for Nashville to pursue a career in music.

For this son, pleasing Dad was important, and fortunately he didn't give up his own dream. However, they would have had a better relationship if Dad had more readily accepted his son's passion.

Parents can support their children's dreams in various ways, according to their emotional and material resources. Here is a dad who did so on a grand scale:

> A teenager had a dream of playing hockey in the Olympic Games. His father, who also had a passion for hockey, bought a skating rink so that the family could combine making a living and supporting the son's dream. Dad hired a coach, who developed a hockey team for his son to play on.

You can honor your child's dream by changing your attitude—this is easier for many of us than buying a skating rink!

> A father had a son who was not doing very well academically. Dad noticed, however, that his son excelled in gymnastics. So instead of pushing the child in his studies, Dad concentrated on helping him feel successful as an athlete. He did not ignore his son's studies, but he focused on what the child did well and encouraged him to pursue his dream.

Show that you believe in your children and support them by going to their school events and teacher conferences, recitals, games, and other activities and by recognizing all areas into which they put effort. Many adults complain that their parents were so busy working that they never had time to pay attention to the important events in their children's lives. Be careful not to let your children's growing-up years slip by without emboldening their dreams every chance you get.

## Genuine Encounter Moments

*Many parents are with their children physically, but mentally their focus is elsewhere. Togetherness without genuine encounter is not togetherness at all.*

—DOROTHY CORKILLE BRIGGS, *YOUR CHILD'S SELF-ESTEEM*

Attentive connections release a powerful hormone in the brain called *oxytocin.* This hormone builds trust, rapport, and bonding. By giving your child focused attention you not only build your child's self-esteem but you are also wiring your child's brain for success in life. It is vital for your child's brain development that you make numerous connections with your child every day. Holding, rocking, cooing, and other means of engaging your infant help promote healthy wiring of the brain.

There are two types of connections or moments you can give young-sters and teens: teachable moments and genuine encounter moments (GEMs). Teachable moments are when you take the time to teach your child something. GEMs have a very different nature. Both types of moments are important.

When your child comes to you to tell you something, do you (1) ignore him or her, (2) pretend to listen, or (3) listen attentively? When you listen attentively, you are having a genuine encounter moment. Here are seven steps for a GEM:

**1. Remove all distractions.** Set down your phone (no peeking at texts), close your laptop, put your magazine down, and so on.

**2. Get on your child's level.** Towering over your child is intimi-dating and less intimate.

**3. Maintain eye contact.** Dopamine is then released in both of your bodies, and this helps you feel bonded and feel good in the other's presence.

**4. Give one hundred percent of your attention.** Do not think about your priority list, what to have for dinner, or the argument you just had with your partner.

**5. Touch.** Touching releases serotonin, a chemical that makes you both feel good.

**6. Let your child lead.** Try to feel what he or she is feeling. We often hijack our child's moments by asking questions or giving unsolicited advice or lectures. Stay present in where the child wants to lead the encounter with you. Making observations about the child and the child's experience is a good way to help him or her feel seen and heard.

**7. Give a response from the heart, not the head.** Responses from the head often lead to disconnection. Heartfelt responses increase your bonding and leave both of you feeling more satisfied. You are also increasing your child's social and emotional intelligence.

It isn't humanly possible for every conversation with your child to be a GEM. However, if you can arrange to have several GEMs each day, you'll see a marked improvement in your relationship and your child's behavior. When children get this kind of attention, they have little need to use misbehavior to get your attention.

If your little one comes to you wanting your attention and you cannot give it immediately, set a timer to indicate to your child when you will be available.

When your child is a teenager it is important to drop what you are doing in order to connect. Teenagers turn toward their peers for connection. They come less frequently to their parents. So when they do come to you to connect, it is important to drop what you are doing to attend to your teen.

A recent survey of one thousand parents found that the average parent spends a mere five hours per week communicating face-to-face with his or her child. Parents blamed this disconnection on their kids spending too much time on their screens, spending too much time in their bedrooms, and inordinate amounts of time on their phones. This amount of disconnection is wreaking havoc on the mental health of our children and our families. The current statistics of teen eating disorders, depression, and suicide are staggering.

Choose not to be one of these statistics. Parenting is arduous and often thankless work. You may not see immediate results. In fact, you may not be fully appreciated until your children have children. But if you live from your values and stick up for your values even when the odds are stacked against you, you will feel more confident and more authentic in your life.

## Take Time to Connect

Cooperation is readily available when we take time to connect. If you need to ask your child to do something, take a few moments to connect prior to asking. For little ones, a few tickles and "chase me" time will suffice. For older children, chatting about something light and fun usually works.

## Spend Alone Time with Each Child

Alone time with a parent is soul time for a child. If you have several children, this may appear to be quite impossible. However, life presents many opportunities to do so: take one child to run errands like grocery shopping, filling up on gas, or going to the hardware store.

A single dad of five girls under the age of eleven I was coaching looked at me in bewilderment when I made this suggestion. "How in the world am I going to do that?" he asked. "I barely get enough time to take a shower in the morning!" After doing some brainstorming, he realized that one of his chores was to walk the dog. He decided that one way he could get some one-on-time with his children was to walk the dog with a different daughter each time. Later he remarked on how much more peaceful his household had become and how he had gotten to know things about each of the girls he never knew before.

## Teach Your Child the Power of a Growth Mindset

Kids acquire either a growth mindset or a fixed mindset. A growth mindset, proposed by Stanford professor Carol Dweck in her book *Mindset*, describes people who believe that their success depends on time, persistence, and effort. Kids with a growth mindset feel that their intelligence is not fixed but is dependent on their efforts. They love a challenge, persist through obstacles, seek criticism, and get inspiration from others' success.

Kids who hold a growth mindset believe that with time, practice, and focused effort they can achieve what they want. These kids are not afraid of failure. Focusing on their process rather than the outcome is one of the key components. Kids with a growth mindset are more engaged and motivated learners.

The opposite, a fixed mindset, sees qualities as fixed traits that cannot change. With a fixed mindset, talent and intelligence are enough to lead to success. Kids with a fixed mindset hold the belief that they are either good or bad at something. For instance, someone with a fixed mindset might say, "I'm a natural-born dancer" or "I'm no good at dancing." These kids may avoid challenges, refuse helpful feedback, and give up easily.

There are six ways to help your child develop a growth mindset.

**1. Teach your child how the brain works.** The brain is a muscle. When you learn new things, parts of your brain get larger, like a muscle. There are many informational YouTube videos on the brain that are helpful.

**2. Help them to identify and change their negative self-talk.** Self-talk is the practice of talking to oneself either out loud or silently. Usually by the time your child is eight, his or her self-talk is more internal. When this is the case, you may have to ask your child what he or she is saying to so you can help redirect the negative self-talk. Your aim is to replace self-talk like "I can't" with "With practice, I can get this." Replace "I don't know how" with "I can ask someone for help," and replace "I'm shy" with "I can talk to one person" and other positive, hopeful messages.

**3. Assist them in practicing their new self-talk when needed.** If negative self-talk is embedded in the way they approach challenging situations, you may need to have children practice the new self-talk until it feels real to them. (See the following example.)

> Snorkeling was not yet in my seven-year-old granddaughter's repertoire. It was her first attempt. She came out of the ocean coughing, spitting, and crying. "This is too hard. I don't like this! Take this off of me!" she said, referring to her snorkel and mask. She flopped on the beach, discouraged.
>
> I knelt beside her and said empathetically, "Learning something new does feel hard sometimes." When she calmed down a bit, I told her about self-talk and how important it is to have an attitude of improving on things and not giving up.
>
> I shared with her my experience of thinking I was bad at technology, which often led me to quit before I got the result I wanted. I told her that I started saying, "With practice, I can get this!" And as a result, I got better and better with technology, and it became more fun.
>
> I prompted her to say those words out loud. Her first words were meek, and it seemed like she didn't believe what she was saying. I had her say this phrase with more passion several times before she seemed empowered by it.
>
> After a few minutes, she went back into the ocean with her mask and snorkel on. By the end of the day, she was having so much fun snorkeling that I had a hard time getting her out of the water!

### 4. Choose encouraging words wisely.

*Everyone knows that a little encouragement goes a long way. But a "little encouragement" needs to be more than the same few phrases repeated over and over again. We all need to have more than the traditional "good job" and "good girl." Sincerity, creativity, and variety are powerful tools in building your child's self-esteem.*

—EDWARD S. KUBANY

Words like "good boy" and "good job" offer external praise and often result in developing children who look to the adult for their source of encouragement rather than developing an internal locus of encouragement. Instead, try using phrases that emphasize personal mastery, independence, character development, their process, self-reflection, strategy, and enjoyment. Here are some possibilities:

- "Just an oops. Take a breath and try again."
- "That was kind."
- "Wow! You focused on that for a long time."
- "Looks like your strategy worked!"
- "You did that all by yourself!"
- "You felt like giving up, but then you persisted, and look what happened!"
- "It looks like you really enjoyed doing that, didn't you?"

**5. Be a healthy role model.** Remember that your kids learn best by your modeling. If they hear you say fixed-mindset words like "I can't do this," "I'm not good at public speaking," or "That was stupid of me," they will begin to mimic your attitudes.

**6. Watch, read, and tell inspiring stories about other achievements that resulted from effort and persistence.** For example, read about Einstein's struggles in his early school days or Jim Carrey, whose family was so poor they lived in a van during his teens.

If you are new to this concept, there are numerous sites on the web that have information on mindsets and posters to hang in your child's room.

A fixed or growth mindset will shape your child's life. Learn to help your child fine-tune this internal monologue to adopt the much more fruitful and nourishing growth mindset.

## Be Mindful of Your Messages

Be careful what messages you give your children and be aware of how they might interpret what you say. For example, one mother frequently and endearingly called her youngest child "baby." Later, she found out the term made him feel small and powerless. Definitely not what she had intended!

Another mother frequently responded to her toddler's requests to carry her by saying, "Honey, you're too heavy." One day her daughter pleaded, "Hold me, Mommy. I'm not too heavy!" Again, a message this mother was not intending!

Ask your children, "How do you feel when I say . . . ?" to make sure they are interpreting your message the way you want them to.

### *Monitor Your Tone of Voice*

Your tone of voice also determines, to a great extent, how cooperative your child is. Keep a light, curious, nonjudgmental tone to your voice. Talk as if you were talking to your best friend. Speak respectfully, which helps your child feel important and competent.

To help you with your tone, ask your partner to create a signal the two of you can use. My husband and I used the word "TV" to gently remind each other when our tone was harsh or demeaning.

## Be Willing to Learn from Your Child

We expect our children to learn from us because we are the adults. However, there is no reason why parents can't learn from their children too. Children have a fresh way of looking at the world. They can amaze us if we are open to learning from them.

> Mom said to seven-year-old Judy, "It's really neat how you go into your room when you're mad. When you come back out, you're ready to talk."
>
> Judy looked at Mom strangely and said, "Yeah, Mom."
>
> A couple of weeks later, Mom and Dad were having a fight. Judy cautiously approached Mom and said, "Sometimes when I'm mad, I

go to my room and think happy thoughts. Then it's not so bad when I come out." Mom and Dad caught each other's eyes and grinned sheepishly. They stopped fighting, and both thought of a different way to handle their altercation.

## Honor Your Child's Intentions

When you speak to children about misbehavior, include words that show you understand what their true intention was. For example, if your daughter pesters the cat, you might say, "You're hurting the cat. I know that is not what you want because you're usually so loving to him. Is there something you want to talk about?" If you say, "Stop hurting the cat," her behavior is likely to be directed toward a new victim or continue in some other way.

Usually, children misbehave unconsciously. When you bring their mistake to their attention in a loving way, they can look at their behavior and decide what to do about it without getting hung up on discouraging self-talk ("I'm bad").

## Express Affection

A major human need is for physical contact with others. Without it, children fail to thrive. Showing your love for your child through physical expression is a powerful way to offer encouragement. Hold a small child on your lap to read or talk or just be. Stoop down to children's level and look at them. Move close to them. Don't yell at them from across the room or the yard. Put your arm around them or on their shoulder. If you have preteens or teenagers who don't want much physical contact, sit near them or allow them to lean over your shoulder. Smile at them to show them you accept and appreciate them. These suggestions might seem unnecessary, but it's amazing how little time we take to do these simple gestures that offer encouragement and can turn a child around.

## Respect Your Child's Boundaries

Some parents are confused about appropriate expression of physical affection, especially now with so many reports about sexual abuse in the news.

It is very important for children's growth and self-esteem to respect their physical and emotional boundaries. When adults don't respect these boundaries, children do not learn how to trust others or to put limits on how other people treat them. They may find it difficult to say no to strangers, to people wanting sexual favors, or to others who wish to take advantage of them in some way. Boys are just as vulnerable as girls, though we hear more often about abuse to girls.

Boundary invasions include the following:

- Entering an older child's bathroom or bedroom without knocking and asking permission
- Forcing affection that the child doesn't want—including kisses and hugs from relatives
- Cleaning up an older child's room without permission
- Forcing a child to eat food he or she doesn't want
- Forcing medicine on a child
- Borrowing money or possessions without permission
- Telling the child's confidences to others without permission (including the other parent)
- Making the child tell private thoughts or give information
- Reading an older child's text messages, diary, or class papers without permission
- Continuing to tickle or roughhouse when the child wants to stop

It may be difficult to tell if a child is really enjoying physical affection, like being tickled or kissed. My children and I developed a signal to indicate when we had had enough. When the tickled person said, "Please stop," the tickler did so immediately. We tried to be cognizant of one another's physical and emotional boundaries.

Even when it is necessary for you to do certain things, such as give medicine, enter a room, or read something, because a child's health and safety depend on it, you can do so respectfully and give advance notice. Sometimes parents unwittingly disrespect a boundary, especially when the child is young.

> Three-year-old James was out with his parents and needed to change his clothes. He didn't want people to see him but there was no place that was private. His dad tried to talk him out of his need for privacy since he was only three. Luckily, Dad realized that he was undermining the lessons he'd been teaching his son about personal safety. He provided a large towel behind which James could change.

> A woman remembers when she broke her leg as a child and the doctors cut off her jeans and underpants to work on her leg. They acted without explaining why or asking her permission to take off her clothes. To this day she recalls how scared and violated she felt.

Children feel safe when adults respect their boundaries—and when adults require other children in the family or classroom to respect their physical and emotional boundaries. Feelings of trust and security are amplified in your home and at school.

## Use Mistakes to Encourage Your Child

Mistakes are a fact of life; we all make them, often. Mastery can be gained only by experience. Experience is defined by the mistakes we make. When your children make a mistake, don't scold them. Their fear of your disapproval will cause them to cover up mistakes, lie, or blame others for their actions. They may also become fearful of taking risks.

It's OK to make mistakes—few of them are fatal—and we learn a great deal about what to do differently next time. Here are five suggestions that minimize the mistake itself and maximize encouragement of your child.

**1. Emphasize what the child can do next time.** Too much concern with what has already happened only encourages excuses and defensiveness from your child. Help your child figure out what to do differently the next time and teach him or her a new skill if he or she needs one.

"Mistakes happen. How could you hold the carton so you won't spill the milk next time?"

**2. Separate the deed from the doer.** Reassure your child that you love him or her, but that you're unwilling to accept inappropriate behavior.

"I don't appreciate you roughhousing at the dinner table but I want you to know that even though I may sound angry, I still love you."

**3. Give your child another chance.** This shows your child you have faith in his or her ability to improve.

"You made a mess while eating in the family room yesterday when you promised you wouldn't make a mess. You may not eat there today, but you can try again tomorrow."

**4. Show your child what to do.** Telling a child what to do repeatedly frustrates both parent and child. Children learn best when adults show them what they want and then ask the child to do the same. Pay attention to your child's preferred learning style. Try to use all three major learning styles each time you teach a new skill: visual (seeing), auditory (listening), and kinesthetic (doing, hands-on).

"Watch how I pour the cereal into the bowl, and then how I pour the milk slowly. See? That way you don't spill any. Now you try."

**5. Ask questions.** Ask questions that encourage your child to figure things out on his or her own. Ask in a loving, accepting tone, "What did you learn from that? What would happen if . . . ?" Your children will learn more when they think of their own solutions than when they listen to yours. This is especially true of teenagers. Questions guide children to think for themselves. Consequently, their feelings of self-reliance increase.

We don't enjoy watching our children fail, so our natural inclination is to offer them all the help they might need. They sense our doubt about their ability to complete things "correctly" without our help. Seek the balance between doing everything for your children on the one hand and letting them fail on the other. Your goal is to encourage them to solve problems themselves and to seek help when they need it.

**6. Teach Children to Repair Mistakes.** Children need to learn to take responsibility for their mistakes. It is important for them to learn how to make amends for a mistake that harms someone or someone's property. Parents can teach by modeling the behavior. If you bump into a car in the parking lot and the owner is not around to demand repair of the mistake, you can bet that your children will take note of whether you leave your name and telephone number or whether you escape as quickly as possible, hoping no one noticed.

Here is an example of repairing mistakes:

A father allowed his children to use his tools to do a project. They got spots of paint on the handles of his tools. The father asked them what they might do to repair their mistake. The kids asked their dad if they could paint all the handles silver. Dad was pleasantly surprised by their solution.

It is important that the person who makes the mistake determine how to make up for it. This make up should not be forced on the child. What is decided must be acceptable to the person who was inconvenienced. Your goal is for your children to learn to think about repairing mistakes on their own. They may need your help to remember if they are young or the skill is new to them.

## Filter Your Child's Experiences

One of our jobs as a parent is to act as a filter for our children's experiences. You want to allow certain experiences and filter out experiences that would overwhelm your children. Among these are abuse of any kind, physical danger, or experiences simply too complex for the child's stage of development. However, it is equally important that we allow challenging experiences into our children's lives. Through challenges they learn to be self-confident. The more often children cope successfully with challenges, the greater their self-esteem and the more competent they feel.

The child in this story faces both an unreasonable experience for her age and a reasonable one. Her mother thoughtfully filters the outcomes of each to maximize her daughter's learning.

> On the day of her departure for her grandparents' house, sixteen-year-old Melissa left her plane ticket on the dresser in her bedroom. Mom happened to see it lying there. She considered the idea of saying nothing, but she felt this natural consequence of a missed plane would be too disappointing for Melissa. So Mom picked up the ticket and handed it to Melissa without saying anything. Melissa sheepishly took the ticket and placed it on the dashboard of the car.
>
> As they walked into the airport, Mom noticed that Melissa had again forgotten the ticket. At this point, Mom realized they were early and would have time to deal with the natural consequence of the forgotten ticket, so she said nothing. Halfway to the ticket counter, Melissa gasped, "Oh my gosh, I forgot my ticket again!" Without critical words or looks, Mom handed the car keys to Melissa, who ran back and retrieved her ticket from the car. (It was a very small airport and Mom could watch her from the window.)

## Provide Order and Routine

The establishment of order and routine in your home develops a sense of security for your children. Routines give children something they can count on. Think of how unsafe and insecure we adults would feel if just one thing in our daily lives changed—we could drive on either side of the road whenever we felt like it. It's also important for children to know, to some degree, what they can expect. They need this stability as a springboard for confidence. Children who don't have order and routine are too often reeling from the last thing that happened to them. They stand little chance of developing a strong foundation of self-confidence.

Bedtime seems to be a particularly difficult time for most parents and one that can go more smoothly with a routine. Everyone is usually tired and stressed by the end of the day, and this only makes matters worse. I have chosen to use bedtime as a specific example to demonstrate how routine can be established in general.

"Zachary, time for bed," announces Mother.

"No!" two-year-old Zachary yelps, running toward the playroom.

Mother follows close behind, pleading, "It's time for bed, honey. Come on, now."

"No, Mommy, no!" Zachary squeals.

As Mother swoops down to pick him up, Zachary's body stiffens, his back arches—making him feel heavy—and he begins wildly kicking his feet to free himself from her tightening grip.

"Stop it! You're going to bed, NOW!" Mother declares, determined to get her struggling child to bed. Zachary begins to cry loudly as Mother, exasperated, pulls off his clothes for his bath. This emotional and physical power struggle continues through bath, pajamas, and teeth brushing, and abruptly ends with a token good night kiss.

Exhausted, Mother sags down the stairs hoping for some peace and quiet, only to hear, "Mommy, drink. Me go potty!" Mother angrily takes Zachary a glass of water and makes a quick trip to the bathroom with him. She sets him on his bed and says through clenched teeth, "Don't let me hear another peep out of you. Good night!"

Mother stomps down the stairs feeling guilty and frustrated.

Now, look at this same scene through Zachary's eyes. Because of our myopic, parental viewpoint, we sometimes miss the opportunity to understand how our child sees things.

Imagine that you are in the middle of a good book and your spouse says, "It's time for bed." Despite your response of "No, I'm not ready just yet," he or she helps you unwillingly up the stairs and forces you to go to bed. Consider how you feel. Do you feel disrespected, violated, angry, or controlled?

You may be thinking, "Yes, but a two-year-old doesn't feel this way. It's not the same; he's not an adult. Besides, I'm the parent." True, the child is not yet an adult. However, he is a person with feelings. He's at an important growth stage: he wants independence and is experimenting with how to have his choices be known and honored.

Bedtime can be a special time for closeness between parents and children. It is natural for us to desire to feel loved and connected before going to sleep. Often, however, parents have overburdened themselves during the day. They're eager to get their children in bed as soon as possible so they can have some quiet time for themselves. Children are likely to feel that their parents are trying to "get rid of them." Our children show that they haven't had enough closeness by repeatedly demanding drinks and potty breaks.

How can you give your children what they want and need and still have them go to bed in a timely manner? Respect your own needs. Take care of yourself during the day so that you're not feeling derailed at your child's bedtime.

Whenever possible, have both parents be a part of the bedtime ritual. Bedtime is more fun and less of a burden when both parents participate.

Start your bedtime ritual forty-five minutes to one hour before your child's actual bedtime hour to avoid unnecessary stress and struggle. This process should be a time for winding down. In other words, eliminate activities that would excite the child, such as roughhousing or tickling. An early bedtime routine also allows you some solitude or "couple time" after your child has gone to bed. Here are some additional things you can do to make bedtime happen smoothly:

**Respect children's sense of time** by telling them when bedtime is in fifteen minutes, allowing them to complete a particular activity before their actual bedtime hour.

**Offer choices instead of orders**. Your children will have a feeling of control over what happens to them when you give them choices. For example, you might say, "Do you want your dad or me to help you with your bath?" or "Do you want to sleep with your gorilla or your kitty?"

**Create a bedtime ritual** with your child's help and advice. For example, read a story, snuggle, say a prayer, give a hug and two kisses, and leave the room singing a song. The routine needs to have a quality of sameness—the same order or the same song for young children—to provide a sense of security.

**Create closeness**. For example, talk about "Remember when," such as, "Remember when we went camping and that raccoon got into our food stash?" or "I remember when you were a little baby and loved to have your tummy rubbed." These conversations set the stage for peaceful sleep without bad dreams.

Say three things that you love about each other. Start each statement with, "What I love about you is . . ." and complete it with a specific thing you love. You might say, "What I love about you is the way your singing lifts my spirits."

Another alternative is to ask the following questions, which allow your child to share more about him- or herself: "What was the best thing that happened to you today?" "What was the worst thing that happened to you today?" "What was the silliest thing that happened to you today?"

Teens may talk more freely with the lights out. Try to discover what encourages your child to communicate with you the most.

Dr. Deepak Chopra's mother was a magnificent storyteller. Every night as she put her kids to bed, she would tell them a bedtime story and stop it with a cliff-hanger. Then she would tell her children that she wanted them to end the story for her the next day. She had two conditions. It needed to end with a love story and have a happy ending. Chopra said that's what most influenced his entire life. He decided the best stories are love stories. He continued this ritual with his own kids.

This next suggestion is only for the brave of heart. As you put your child to bed, ask him or her to rate you as a parent that day from zero being the worst to ten being the best. And then ask how you could improve. Beware. There were some days I got a below-zero rating! Whatever your rating, ask what you did or didn't do to get that rating.

You can find out some valuable information to improve your parenting skills. As my children grew older, they frequently asked me to rate them as my child. These moments were revealing and very precious.

After you have completed your bedtime routine, leave your child's room. Explain once when you start this new bedtime routine, "If you come out of your room for any reason other than an emergency, I will lovingly guide or carry you back to your room. I will not talk to you after saying good night and closing your bedroom door."

It's important that you not talk to your child after the bedtime routine is complete. If you continue to talk with your child, you are more likely to start negotiating or engaging in a power struggle. You may have to guide your child back to his or her room several times, particularly at the beginning because children will test you. However, as the week progresses, bedtime will become more pleasant for both you and your child.

You can make bedtime a time of nurturing, closeness, shared communication, and fun. By involving your children in the decision-making process and spending this special time with them, they will feel valued and respected. Order and routine offer your children security because they learn they can depend on certain events consistently occurring.

If you are still having trouble after implementing some of these methods, check to see if you are truly present. It is impossible to fill our child's cup if you are mentally elsewhere. Or your child might have additional needs you are unaware of: a weighted blanket, soft music, a night-light, or your permission to read in bed after you leave are only a few ideas.

Routines are important to establish for other activities such as:
- Waking up
- Getting dressed
- Getting children off to school
- Picking them up from school
- Homework
- Doing chores

## Keep Work Lighthearted

Nagging and scolding our children about doing their chores is not fun for anyone. The more fun and lighthearted you can be about doing chores increases your odds of winning your children's cooperation.

> My husband likes a tidy house. After meeting with great resistance from the rest of us, he came up with a delightful way to win our cooperation. Every night before bed we would all pick up for ten minutes. My husband set the timer and put on lively music, and we all dashed around picking up as much as we could. When the timer went off, we stopped. Then we celebrated what we had accomplished.

How can you start making chores more fun? Elicit your child's help in finding new, innovative ways to get your household chores done.

## Avoid These Common Parenting Pitfalls

Following is a list of common parental mistakes. Many of these are very familiar to me because I have made them more than once. As you read them, remember to be kind to yourself. We are all having to learn new ways of disciplining our children for this twenty-first century. Work consciously to throw these mistakes out of your parenting toolbox.

### Hassle over Minor Issues

I am sure you have heard the old adage "Pick your battles." Children learn to ignore micromanaging parents. Work on one correction at a time until you achieve success. Ask yourself, "Is this really important?" If not, address the issue later rather than working on too many things at one time.

### Use Humiliation to Motivate

"You're not going to manipulate me this time, young lady. It's your fault you forgot your T-shirt," sniped a mother publicly at her daughter. The daughter lowered her head in shame and slumped away.

Perhaps you grew up in a home where humiliation was used in an attempt to motivate. If that is true, you may be prone to using this method. Hurt people usually hurt people. This technique might get the behavior you wish momentarily, but you lay the groundwork for vengeance and mistrust. It is especially harmful when you use it in front of your child's friends.

> Simon had a crush on a girl at school and shared his secret with his mom. Later that day, when Simon was with his friends, Mom teased him about her. His friends then proceeded to tease him too. Simon was deeply embarrassed and decided it wasn't safe for him to share with his mom the matters of his heart.

Ultimately, we want to be a safe haven for our kids to share their secrets and be available to them when they need us. If you are feeling brave, ask your child if there is anything you do that makes you an unsafe parent.

## Use Criticism to Motivate

Research tells us that the average child receives 432 negative comments per day and just 32 positive ones. Scary thought, isn't it? Avoid criticism and disapproval. Respond to your children in a way that helps them feel encouraged. Give them constructive messages.

> A school principal requires that teachers send five children to his office for good behavior before they can send one for misbehavior. His policy has changed the way his teachers think about their students.

An elementary teacher once called Rudolf Dreikurs, MD, the well-known psychiatrist, into her classroom. She began to complain to Dr. Dreikurs about a child's poor handwriting, in front of the child. "Look at this mess. Have you ever seen such horrible penmanship? You can't read a thing on this whole paper!"

Dr. Dreikurs studied the paper and then smiled at the child. "I don't know . . . that's a pretty nicely shaped *O* right there," he said, pointing at the only legible letter on the page. His encouraging comment provided the motivation for the child to work on his penmanship, whereas all the teacher's criticism had not.

## Overuse of the Words "No" and "Don't"

How many times a day do you say the words "no" or "don't"? No one likes to hear the word "no." Many times, we say these words about things that don't really matter. Here are some alternative ways to say no:

1. "That's not an option."
2. "I am unwilling . . ."
3. Say it in a funny way, such as, "Never in a million trillion years!"
4. Sing, "No, no, no."
5. "That's not appropriate."
6. "I am not ready for you to do that yet."
7. For younger children, use distraction.
8. Ask, "What do you think you would need to do before I would be willing to say yes to that?"
9. Ask, "What do you think? Is this a good choice for you?" (If you choose to use this, make sure you are willing to abide by their answer.)
10. "No, but I would be willing to . . ."
11. Ask, "What are your other options?"
12. For youngsters who have something you don't want them to have, say, "That's not a toy. However, this is a toy you can play with."
13. "I appreciate your asking. However . . ."
14. Give them an alternative. "Walls are not for coloring. Here is a piece of paper."
15. Tell them what to do instead, such as, "Water needs to stay in the tub."
16. "This is not negotiable."
17. "Yes, as soon as [task] is done."
18. "I'd love to, but now's not an option. Let's go put it on my calendar."

Next time you need to say no, choose a more creative way from this list or make up one of your own.

I am not suggesting that you never say no directly. It is important that children hear that word so they can learn how to adjust.

## *Use Comparison or Competition to Motivate*

Comparison of one person to another breeds competition. Competition pits person against person and makes each feel like he or she must be better than the other. This is a hopeless situation because there will always be one person who can do something better than another.

The child who is taught cooperation instead of competition will be happiest and have the versatility to survive in our world. People who must always try to prove themselves will never be at peace.

We often instigate bickering and competition among our children when we say things like, "Whoever gets to the car first gets to ride shotgun."

Today's managers are looking for people who can "play nicely" on a team. Your family is the first team your child will play on. Set your child up for success by asking yourself, "How can I make this activity a team effort?"

## *Be Overprotective*

When parents overprotect children, they send the message that life is dangerous, and children can't handle it. Children need suitable opportunities to struggle with figuring out how to deal with the challenges they face. Through struggling, they learn how to adjust when life throws them curveballs. They learn resilience and gain confidence in their abilities to take care of themselves (self-reliance).

> I invited a friend's eight-year-old son to go swimming with my son. Todd had chronic ear infections and had to use earplugs. He asked me to put them in for him, as his mother always did. I smiled and touched his shoulder lovingly and said, "I think you can figure out how to do it."

As he whined and complained, I remained silent. Finally, he began to struggle with the earplugs. After dropping them, putting them in upside down, and so on, he at last succeeded. I checked that they were in properly, and the pride he obviously felt was great to see!

# 3

# Concentrate on Teaching Life Skills

**M**isbehavior happens when children don't have the right skills to handle the present situation. For example, when your children are fighting, you may yell, "Stop fighting!" This is not very useful if you haven't taught your children how to negotiate. Instead of thinking, *How can I get my child to stop this behavior?* think, *What skill can I teach and/or have my child practice right now?* Here are eleven essential life skills you may want to consider. If you have already done some of the things on the list, pat yourself on the back. If there are some new tips you haven't thought about, work on them slowly so as not to overwhelm yourself and your child. Remember, you have eighteen years to work on them!

## Self-Efficacy

Self-efficacy is the belief in one's own ability to do something.

### *Things to Do*

- Let your children fail early on in life so they learn that failure is simply a part of life.
- Discuss your own failures and hardships. Share what you learned, how you grew, and what you did to get yourself through the situations.

- Celebrate failures in your family.
- Place a high value on education, either in the system and/or self-learning.
- If your children are struggling and want to quit, suggest that they do one more. Or if they are struggling in an extracurricular activity and want to quit, have them finish the term. Then let them choose another activity.
- Teach them the importance of healthy self-talk and how to monitor it.
- Practice the concept of perseverance.
- Allow your child to struggle. Avoid rushing in to protect your child from failures. Whatever we protect we make weak.
- Don't do for your children what they can do for themselves.
- Encourage your children to take on new challenges.

## Self-Determination

The skill of self-determination involves feeling able to determine your own fate or course of action without outside influence.

### *Things to Do*

- When your children are presented with a problem, ask them what their options are to handle it. Encourage them to think of many options, so that they know that their choices are unlimited.
- Ask them what outcome they want when they do a project.
- Do not take on the job of making them happy.
- Help them to understand that their choices have consequences that could affect them for a lifetime.
- Explore meanings children attach to events so they don't get stuck in limiting beliefs.
- Do not feel sorry for your child.
- Eliminate all talk of victim mentality in your home.
- Teach them how money works, including interest and compound interest.

## Self-Discipline

Self-discipline involves the training to accomplish a certain task or to adopt a particular pattern of behavior, even if one would rather be doing something else.

### *Things to Do*

- Teach your children about making lists of things they need to get done. Teach them to prioritize the list.
- Let them see you prioritize your day or manage your time and ask for their advice about your list.
- Ask them, "What is your plan?" and then coach them (not advise them—there is a difference!) on their plan. Or ask, "How will you get from here to there (end goal)?"
- Teach them time management skills.
- Assist them in organizing their space.
- Teach them the long-term benefits of learning to do things immediately, completely, and willingly.
- Extol the benefits of routines and habits, including manners, study, and hygiene. Because established habits tend to be automatic, routines become *more* likely to be followed. It takes a mental effort *not* to follow your usual routine.
- Teach them how to break down a task into manageable "bite-size pieces."
- Teach them to have a plan A, plan B, and plan C.

## Self-control

Teaching self-control helps children learn to delay immediate gratification.

### *Things to Do*

- Help your children to think before they act.
- Teach them how to focus and channel their energy.

- Emphasize the importance of putting off immediate gratification in lieu of the benefits of a higher goal.
- Help them understand that their behaviors have consequences, and they are responsible for their actions.
- Do not cave to your children's wanting immediate gratification.
- Teach them how to self-calm. (More on that in a later chapter.)
- Model self-control in your words and actions.
- Play games that require them to be patient and wait their turn.
- Arrange for them to save their money and pay for certain things out of their account.
- Discuss the effect of their behavior in the long term, for example, "What do you think will happen if you continue to . . . ?"

**Note:** the difference between self-disciple and self-control is that self-discipline says *go* and *keep going* and self-control says *no* or *wait*.

## Integrity

Integrity is your agreement and constant alignment with your own values, dreams, goals, and hopes.

### *Things to Do*

- Teach accountability by keeping your agreements.
- Help children to determine whether they are saying something because it is true for them, or if they are saying what they think someone else wants to hear—or saying something to get others off their back.
- Emphasize the value of doing a job well.
- Teach them how to repair their mistakes to restore trust in themselves and others.
- Teach them to say no respectfully.
- When children have completed a chore or project, ask them if they gave it their hundred percent, understanding that is difficult to give a hundred percent all the time. Help them to determine when and where to give a hundred percent.

- Help them understand the sacredness of having someone's trust, how easy it is to destroy it, and how difficult it is to reestablish it.
- Model keeping your word or changing the agreement when necessary.

## Self-Reflection

Help your children develop the ability to reflect and understand their thoughts and actions.

### Things to Do

- Ask your children in a nonjudgmental tone, "What happened? How did it happen? What was your part in this problem? Why do you think you did that? Was it helpful? What is one thing you could do differently next time?"
- Ask questions about their body: "How does your body feel when _____ happens? What does your body need?"
- Encourage them to learn to love feedback, correction, and criticism.
- Teach them to be aware of their own limits.
- Help them to be able to recognize and express their needs and desires.

**Warning:** if your child is unwilling to self-reflect, check your tone of voice to make sure it is curious and accepting.

## Self-Acceptance

Kids need to develop an acceptance of self despite any perceived deficiencies.

### Things to Do

- Use encouragement instead of praise.
- Let your children know that *everyone* has strengths and weaknesses.
- Teach your children to honor and respect other people's differences.
- Model the courage to be imperfect.

- Talk about your mistakes or limitations in an accepting way.
- Don't allow you children to criticize themselves or others.
- Be patient with your children.
- Celebrate their mistakes.
- Help develop a growth mindset.

## Self-Advocacy

The ability to understand and effectively communicate one's needs to other individuals is self-advocacy. There are three steps to becoming an effective self-advocate:

1. **Know yourself.** For example, children might discover that they are easily distracted at school.
2. **Know what you need.** They may need to sit in the front row at school.
3. **Know how to get what you need.** Here are some areas to work on:
   - Make good eye contact.
   - Make a request without blaming or complaining.
   - Listen to and understand the other person's point of view.
   - Negotiate for what they want and need.
   - Do not give up when roadblocks occur—for example, if the other person gets intimidating.
   - Know when, how, and whom to ask for help.
   - Be resourceful. If that person or situation doesn't work, ask children, "What else can you try?"

### *Things to Do*

- Let children make their own appointments with the dentist, doctors, and veterinarian as soon as they are capable.
- Make a list of questions to ask the dentist or doctor before their appointments.

- Include your children in parent-teacher conferences. Discuss their needs for their learning before the conference. Support your children while they ask for what they need.
- If your children are having a problem with a coach, teacher, Boy or Girl Scout leader, and so on, have them role-play with you. Before they address the person, have them practice with you being the person they need to address. Be willing to go with them to the meeting.
- Have them politely order for themselves at restaurants.
- Encourage them to fill out their own paperwork, for example, field trip forms, doctor's questionnaires.

## Self-Respect

Help your children develop pride in their self, a feeling that they are operating with honor and dignity.

### *Things to Do*

- Don't allow children to put themselves down.
- Role-play with your children how to set clear boundaries with others.
- Assist your children in making good friend choices.
- Encourage them to develop their own opinions and interests.
- Many TV shows are full of characters who depreciate self and others. Monitor what your children watch and how much they watch. Have discussions about what they saw if you choose to let them watch these shows.
- Teach them to be authentic in their responses to you, teachers, and friends.
- Model being authentic.

## Critical Thinking

Teach your children how to analyze and evaluate information to guide their beliefs, decisions, and actions.

- Learn to ask powerful questions rather than giving advice or assuming you know. Your tone of voice must come from a place of curiosity rather than judgment or you risk shutting down your child.

    1. How did that happen?
    2. How do feel about this?
    3. What outcome are you looking for?
    4. What is your strategy? Is it working?
    5. What are your resources?
    6. What are three different ways you could have handled that situation?
    7. Play the "What would you do if . . ." game. Or "What would happen if . . . ?"

- Ask their opinion or ask for advice often.
- Have them evaluate their answers rather than tell them what is right or wrong.
- Involve them in creating solutions to problems. Family meetings are the ideal place to do this.
- Invite them to pretend they are detectives and have them solve the mystery.
- Teach them how to think, not what to think.
- Read books together and ask them what they think will happen next or what the character's next best move would be.
- Play games that involve thinking ahead and strategizing,

## Communication

Develop the skill of determining what one wants to communicate and realizing how it will be understood by others.

- Practice saying, "This is what I heard you say [repeat what you thought you heard]. Is that right? Did I miss anything?"
- Ask children to repeat what they heard you say.
- Ask children, "What do you need?"

- Express your needs freely.
- Help children to identify their feelings.
- Allow expression of all feelings.

Teachers and employers feel communication skills are lacking today. The prevalence of texting and e-mailing today, along with the new social difficulties resulting from the COVID-19 pandemic, have interfered with the development of effective communication skills.

## Parent with the End in Mind

Parents have the responsibility to prepare their children for adulthood. Some techniques, such as overpowering children, look for the expedient solution to solve problems in the short run but fail to help the child learn. Giving insufficient time or having too little patience causes problems for children that they must deal with in adulthood. Stop using short-term fixes. Decide to invest in your child's future. This will pay off for you too. You can avoid the rebellious teen, the adult child who suffers the failure-to-launch syndrome, or the adult child who doesn't want anything to do with you.

As you parent your children, ask yourself:

- What will my children learn from this discipline?
- Will it help them develop characteristics they need as an adult?
- Will it teach the essential life skills they need to live a successful and fulfilling adult life?

# 4

# What Is Your Parenting Style?

**M**ost parents use one of four common parenting styles or, perhaps, a blend of two. It is helpful to define these styles here so that you can determine what form of discipline you use most often and decide if you wish to continue with that method or exchange it for something more effective. The parenting styles I refer to are autocratic, permissive, absentee, and authoritative.

## Autocratic Parenting

> Jason's report card has a D on it. His dad sees it and yells, "No son of mine is going to get Ds on his report card! You're grounded for two weeks. Now get in your room and study!"

Autocratic parents view children and situations as bad or wrong. They use force as the discipline tool to manipulate their children to do what they want. Force includes guilt, threats, punishment, grounding, spanking, sarcasm, criticism, intimidation, humiliation, withdrawal of love, commands (not related to immediate safety), bribes, and other attempts to control or make children do something against their will. All these methods diminish children's spirit, self-esteem, and self-confidence. Excessive use of force teaches your child that bullying others works.

Force, or coercive power, motivates through fear instead of love. Fear makes children feel they are not "good enough." A moment's reflection will remind you of times when you have felt the effect of coercive power in your adult life—you understand how destructive it can be.

Fear used as a motivator causes children to protect themselves by lying, hiding themselves, and blaming others. Fear leads to competition, fighting, separation from others, and hostility. Fear of punishment also causes children to give up who they are to become what someone else wants them to be—or rebel against what the authority figure wants. The child's behavior is controlled by an outside source (parent, teacher), rather than by the child's own sense of what is right or wrong. Punishment doesn't develop self-responsibility in children, nor does it show them how to develop their own moral standards. Their internal guidance system (IGS) becomes warped. As a result, children often develop "get away with" or "get by" attitudes.

## Illusion of Effectiveness

Coercive force may immediately cause your child to stop the behavior you object to; however, its effectiveness is only a temporary illusion. The technique "works" for the moment but doesn't promote the learning you wish to see in the long run.

When you use punishment, children become either compliant or resistant and revengeful. After being punished, children often focus on getting even with you rather than thinking about the consequences of their inappropriate behavior and what they needed to learn from their behavior. Children usually respond to coercion in an equally coercive manner by sulking, being uncooperative, becoming uncommunicative, picking on younger siblings or pets, getting bad grades at school, destroying their own property or yours, running away from home, or "forgetting" to do chores. The list of negative reactions is as long as children are creative.

As parents, our response to such behavior is usually more coercion, resulting in an escalation of the child's behavior. Everyone's self-concept is damaged; there is much tension, and a lack of respect and cooperation pervades our home. We say and do things we wish we could edit out of our lives. Guilt and frustration ensue.

## *Obedience Versus Responsibility*

A confusion parents have is the distinction between obedience and responsibility. On rare occasions, children must be obedient for their own safety. A small child must stop at the curb, get away from the hot stove, or stay back from a body of water.

Beyond issues of safety, it is more important that children learn to be responsible in light of the demands of the situation than obedient to an authority figure. By this statement, I mean that children need to learn to think about situations and use their reasoning ability to arrive at the best course of action. This takes problem-solving ability, brainstorming (creativity), and awareness of feelings. If you demand blind obedience from children, you are limiting their ability to learn how to act responsibly.

Parents who use force do so mostly because that's how they were parented. Other parents use it when they are anxious about some stress in their life: a conflict with a spouse or at work, too little time for themselves, financial distress, addition of an elderly parent, or illness in the family. If a child defies you at such a time, you feel even more powerless, and the quick fix of a swat, time-out, taking away a privilege, or grounding seems more efficient.

Yet other parents use force because they believe children must be "taught a lesson" or punished in order to learn how to behave. Research clearly states that these forms of discipline are ineffective.

> *The day the power of love overrules the love of power, the world will know peace.*
> —MAHATMA GANDHI

Check in with yourself the next time you punish your child with force. Ask yourself these questions:

- Am I angry, do I want to hurt back, do I feel powerless?
- Do I want my children to do what I ask to make them (a) be a better person, or (b) obey me?

- Do I want to control my children, or would I rather teach them to control themselves?
- Am I using fear or love to motivate my children?
- What do I want my children to learn right now?
- How can I teach what I want them to learn without using force (being coercive)?

Someday in the future, the use of spanking and other forms of physical force will be as archaic as women not being allowed to vote or Black people being forced to sit in the back of the bus.

Relationships are not built on control but on loving communication.

## Researched Reasons for Avoiding Physical Force to Discipline Children

1. Use of physical force (corporal punishment) says that fear, pain, intimidation, and violence are acceptable methods of resolving conflicts between people, no matter what their age.

2. Physical force is unnecessary. There are many nonviolent disciplinary alternatives that are more effective and pose no risk or harm to children.

3. Physical force confuses discipline with punishment. Discipline is used to teach, while punishment is used for purposes of control and retribution. Young children do not commit crimes that require punishment. Their mistakes call for discipline, that is, teaching a more appropriate response.

4. Physical force inhibits better means of communication and problem-solving. People who use it make little effort to learn nonviolent ways.

5. Physical force confuses love and violence. Children get the impression that violence can be an expression of love. True love is expressed in much healthier, nonviolent ways.

6. Physical force only controls the symptom of a problem. It does not address the problem and, in fact, makes the problem worse.

7. Physical force is dangerous. It can escalate into battering and sometimes results in death. It is very likely to result in physical, mental, spiritual, or emotional harm.

8. Research has shown that physical force increases aggressiveness in children and contributes to vandalism in schools and on the streets. Violence leads to more violence.

9. Physical force reduces a child's ability to concentrate, making it harder for him or her to learn.

10. Physical force denies your child a right to equal protection under the law—a right guaranteed to all citizens in the United States in Section I of the Fourteenth Amendment to the Constitution of the United States.

*Adapted from* Spare the Rod *by Phil E. Quinn (Abingdon Press, 1988).*

## Punished by Rewards

*If people are good only because they fear punishment, and hope for reward, then we are a sorry lot indeed.*
—ALBERT EINSTEIN

Dad sees the D on Jason's report card. He says, "If you bring that grade up to a B, I'll give you ten dollars."

Giving love and material things as a reward and using them to bribe children to get them to behave inevitably backfires. Rewards can be just as controlling as punishment. Children who receive rewards can become dependent on the authority figure for the initiative to accomplish a task. Rewards do not ultimately change behavior. Many parents are confused about this. As with punishment, if the person giving the reward is not around, the child is not motivated to behave. Another problem is that the rewards need to get bigger or better for them to effect behavioral changes.

Material rewards change the motive for which your children do something and the attitude with which they do it. If you ask your children to do things with a reward attached, they begin expecting a reward for simply behaving appropriately. They do not develop a sense of accomplishment and self-satisfaction, which should become their guiding force.

Rewards can interfere with the development of a sense of self-worth. Children may interpret being rewarded to mean they don't need to do anything until there is something in it for them. A sense of worthwhileness comes when we do something for someone else and expect nothing in return. Our culture, though, emphasizes things as the source of good feeling, and children are influenced by this. It is easy for such children to cop a "What's in it for me?" attitude.

> There was an incident where people were outraged at a gas station attendant. On the street in front of the gas station, a man's car caught on fire. Flames engulfed the dashboard. The driver was frantically trying to put the fire out with his coat. The gas station attendant arrived on the scene with a fire extinguisher and said to the driver, "For twenty dollars I'll let you use my fire extinguisher."

True giving is food for the soul. If you rely on rewards to teach children how to behave, you deny them the opportunity to learn to act from internal motivation.

Most people work for a reward—a paycheck. Were it not for that paycheck, many adults would not do the work they do. The paycheck does allow them to support themselves and their families. However, people who do work that gives them satisfaction beyond the money are happier, healthier, and more productive than those who dislike their job. That's because substantial work gives a person a feeling of self-worth and internal satisfaction—the attributes parents wish to develop in children.

Research indicates that rewards do help to encourage certain behaviors. Giving children a star can be an effective incentive to motivate a child initially. But once the new habit is instilled, the reward should be removed quickly. Rewards are most effective when additional connection time with a parent is used rather than material things. For example, the child who gets five stars a week gets to have an additional "date" with a parent.

Entitlement is an epidemic caused by rewards, overdoing, and over-indulging your child. This is a birthday scenario some of you may have experienced:

> After an exorbitant party including a bounce house, a surprise appear-ance from Mickey Mouse, a piñata full of candy, goody bags, and an elaborately decorated cake, it is now time to open the presents. The child rips into one present after another as the parent sits next to her, coaxing her to politely say thank you. The child glances up at the gift giver, barely making eye contact, and mumbles something that has the semblance of gratitude.
>
> The child, who is immersed in discarded ribbons and wrappings, moves quickly to rip open the next gift. Mother internally cringes at her child's behavior but continues her forced smile at the guests. I imagine every parent feels her pain. But nothing changes: one of them will host the next "over the top" birthday because this has now become the norm in this social group.

This extravaganza is but one way parents unwittingly cultivate entitled children. We love our children. We love to see our children's faces light up with delight when they get that perfect gift or when we drop whatever we are doing to accommodate their happiness and comfort.

But here are some indicators of entitlement:
- Children lose their sense of gratitude.
- Interest in "me" becomes more important than "you" or "us."
- Polite requests go by the wayside and irritating demands take their place.
- When things go awry, blame takes precedent over responsibility and proactivity.
- Children feel like rules don't apply to them.

- They rarely help or take initiative for the greater good.
- Deep satisfaction is never experienced as they look for their next "fix."
- The acquisition of things trumps building character.
- Finding their true meaning or purpose in life is difficult.
- They frequently expect to be entertained and say, "I'm bored."
- Whatever you do, it is never enough.

This may be hard to hear as parents who feel like they are making a huge investment in their child's future. However, if you see several of the symptoms discussed above, it is time to make a change.

Children also learn to be entitled when parents are child centered rather than value centered.

> A seven-year-old was lying on the couch watching TV while her mom was busy working in the kitchen. The little girl called out, "Mom, bring me an apple." Mom brought her the apple, but as Mom was on her way back to the kitchen the daughter whined, "You didn't cut it right!" Mom dutifully brought the apple back to the kitchen and cut the apple just the way her daughter liked it. A short time later the child piped up, "Mom, bring me a glass of water." There was never a please or thank-you in the child's demands.

This mom's life was centered around the child. It was not centered around the values of politeness, taking someone else into consideration, or developing self-reliance. An occasional incident is not a problem. We like doing things for our kids. However, daily doses of being catered to can have long-term repercussions.

## Permissive Parenting

> Jason shows Dad the D on his report card. Dad says, "It's OK, son. You'll do better next time."

If rewards and punishments aren't the ways to discipline children, does that mean we should let them do whatever they wish?

Permissive parenting may take the form of not caring about children's grades, who their friends are, where they are, what time they get home, or giving in when the situation calls for firmness or difficult conversations. Permissiveness makes children feel like you don't care, even when you do, and as a result, they may seek care and concern from other people. Teenagers who are hungry for affection and connection often turn to sex, drugs, social media, or gangs to get their needs met. What they want, even though they seem to want you to think otherwise, is guidance, limits, and attention.

Being permissive and indulgent with children causes them to disrespect their parents and themselves. When you allow your children to take advantage of you, it tears away at their self-esteem. Children really do not like to be permitted to act out. Sometimes we parents are permissive because we don't want to deal with conflict. If we let our children do what they want, we avoid conflict at that moment, but in the long run we create a bigger problem that we'll have to deal with later.

Permissive parents also do not teach their children the skills they need to live a fulfilled life. Children's misbehaviors provide opportunities for many lessons on how to do things differently. If you let misbehavior go unnoticed or do not deal with it directly, you deprive your children of valuable information. Such disregard may not be intentional, but it is the effect of permissive parenting.

Mom got the message every parent dreads from the high school: her fifteen-year-old daughter, Jessica, had missed five days of school. When Mom quizzed Jessica about this message, her daughter told her that the student taking attendance had made a mistake; there was no problem. Mom was relieved to hear this because she couldn't imagine her smart, responsible Jessica skipping class.

Two weeks later Jessica started acting tired and irritable. When her mom questioned her, Jessica assured Mom that she was studying a lot and was just tired. Mom felt uneasy but didn't want to give her daughter the message that she didn't trust her, so she said nothing more.

Over time, Jessica became rebellious, uncooperative, and argumentative. The calls from the school's automated messenger became more frequent, though Jessica's grades were still Bs. Life at home was very unpleasant, with Mom alternately asking what was going on or thinking the problems would disappear when Jessica outgrew this "stage." Then one day Jessica told her mom that she was pregnant and had not been going to school much for some time.

This mother has a permissive parenting approach—she does not set clear limits and wants to avoid conflict. She is not effective or assertive enough in investigating the facts behind Jessica's symptoms. Even though she loves her daughter, she fails to be the strong, involved parent this child needs in her teen years.

Alicia, age fourteen, came home from a sleepover bald. Mom didn't know if she wanted to be bald or if the girls had bullied her into shaving her head. But Mom didn't ask because she was afraid to confront Alicia.

Dare to run the risk of a teen's emotional blackmail barrage. This includes eye-rolling, the silent treatment, wall punching, door slamming, and name-calling. Confronting issues requires that you don't take children's behavior personally, which is hard to do. Try to imagine that you have a shield of Teflon in front of you. When injurious words or actions fly at you, imagine them sliding off you and not sticking.

Courage in the face of pain and a willingness to keep coming back when your attempts fail are also necessary. You may be thinking, "Why on earth would I want to bother addressing this hostility?" There are several reasons. Number one is that your teen needs you to. See this behavior as a cry for help. If you don't, his or her behavior is likely to escalate to get your attention. A second reason for you to discuss the hard issues is that you will be less afraid to deal with other people in your life who try to intimidate you.

The old adage "No guts, no glory" is still true in parenting today. Being vulnerable is often required to surmount relationship difficulties.

Tyler was a teen and wanted to spend his time with his friends and less time with me, which was on par for his stage of development. I wanted to blame him by saying something like, "You're never home. Why can't you stay home tonight for a change?" Instead, I risked being rejected by being vulnerable. I said, "I need some Mom time with you. I miss you." I did feel the "glory" when we spent the night on the couch watching a movie and eating popcorn.

It feels much easier to complain and blame rather than stretch yourself to be vulnerable. However, it is hard to resist someone who dares to be vulnerable.

The permissive parenting style leaves the child with an ache, a pain, an emptiness inside. Some describe it as feeling disconnected or having a hole inside. Self-destructive behavior such as addiction can often result in an attempt to assuage these feelings.

## Absentee Parenting

Jason gets a D on his report card. However, neither parent cares or is present to give their son the guidance he needs.

Absentee parenting describes parents who abdicate their parental responsibilities to another parent or school. Jason is likely to feel neglected and unloved and to develop the attitude of "No one else cares so why should I!"

## Authoritative Parenting

Jason shows Dad the D on his report card. Dad asks, "How do you feel about the D?"

"Not so good," replies Jason.

"Yeah, I'll bet that was discouraging. [Pause] What would you like that grade to be?" Dad asks.

"I hate fractions," pouts Jason. "They're stupid!"

"Yes, fractions can feel challenging," Dad empathizes. "Any thoughts about how you can get the help you need?"

"I don't know," Jason responds despondently.

"How about if I help you build that skateboard ramp you've been wanting to build? That will give you some practice with those tough fractions," proposes Dad.

"Wow, when can we get started?" Jason asks enthusiastically.

You can see that authoritative parenting takes more effort initially. Authoritative parenting is based on the use of authentic power. It does not judge a child as wrong or bad but allows you to connect and bond with your child. Using authentic power, you seek to understand rather than judge, to love unconditionally, to build positive self-concepts, and to make sure everyone wins.

Authentic power is not power over or power under but rather a shared power. When parents use authentic power, everyone feels empowered, parent and child alike. These parents inspire children by paying attention to feelings, needs, and desires. They help children develop control from inside themselves, maintained by the children's own set of internalized values. Children learn responsibility and behave in ways that they feel are right for him. Children learn to listen quietly for inner guidance.

Use of authentic power also teaches children that they are their own source of happiness. Children parented in this way experience closeness, respect, cooperation, joy, and awareness.

Mutual respect is a major part of authoritative parenting. If your children do not feel respected by you, it's unlikely that they'll respond to your attempts to win their cooperation. Respect from your children can no longer be demanded or expected in our present time; it must be earned. The best way to get children to respect your rights is to respect theirs. For instance, if you want your children to knock on your door before entering your bedroom, then show them respect by knocking before entering their room.

It takes careful thought to parent in a authoritative way, as this story demonstrates:

I drove four tiring hours to visit my stepdaughters. My husband and young son, Tyler, had driven down before me to meet up with the girls.

As I drove up, my husband and one of his daughters were getting out of the van, on their way to the house. I hugged them both and asked, "Where's Tyler?" They told me he was still in the van. I went to the van to give him a hug too, and was greeted with, "Why did you hug her first?"

I said, "Sounds like you need someone to hold you and love on you."

Tyler said despondently, "Yeah, they don't like me; I hate it here."

I affirmed, "When you're at home, you get Brian all to yourself. But when you come here, you not only have to share him, but it also feels like the girls don't like you. Sometimes I feel that way too."

Tyler was somewhat relieved that he wasn't alone. "You do?" he asked.

I asked, "Why do you think they may have a hard time accepting us?"

Tyler responded, "Because they might feel like we take their daddy away."

"Probably," I agreed, as I held him closely.

He stayed in my arms for a few moments and then said, "OK, let's go inside."

Consider how this story might have turned out if I had used coercive force (as sometimes happens when I'm stressed). I might have responded in this way:

"Why didn't you hug me first?" demands Tyler.

"Because I didn't know you were still in the van. Now, hurry up, we've got to go inside," I answer sternly.

Tyler says, "I don't want to go in. They don't like me."

"Tyler, get your shoes on and let's go," I demand.

"I'm not going in, and you can't make me!" Tyler asserts.

Exasperated, I say, "Fine, just stay in the van! I'm going in," leaving both of us feeling angry and unloved.

It is so easy to use coercive force because that's how many of us were parented. Yet it seldom gives us the satisfaction that we're all seeking in our relationships.

## *How to Become an Authoritative Parent*

Here are some tips to help you convert coercive force into authentic power:

1. When in doubt about what to do, back off. Don't force the issue. Admit to yourself that coercive force is not going to get the results you desire: connection and cooperation.

2. Realize that your children are not "bad" and have not done something "wrong." They simply are, just like you are. When you misbehave, it's not because you're bad or wrong, but because you aren't getting a need met. Give your children the same respect for their needs that you want for yours.

3. Ask yourself, "How would I have liked my parent to have handled a similar situation when I was young?"

4. Use the positive alternatives to coercive force that are discussed in this book. Brainstorm solutions with your partner or coworkers. Watch other parents discipline their children and watch their children's reactions.

5. Try one positive alternative and acknowledge yourself if you were successful. If you fail to get the result you want, ask yourself what you could do differently next time. Keep trying.

6. Eliminate stress as much as you can. Have you ever noticed that when you are stressed you are more likely to snap or use other modes of force with your child?

7. Attend parenting classes, read personal growth books, or get a coach or a therapist so you can move toward loving yourself, your child, your partner, and others in your life unconditionally.

8. Do not get discouraged if you don't succeed immediately in parenting in a new way. Most of us need practice before we can change our ways. Some things are easy to do right away, and some take a lot of practice. If you get discouraged, you're likely to give up.

When you are making changes, there is a transitional phase where you often vacillate between the old and the new until the new behavior becomes more prevalent. During this time, it is easy to beat yourself up for knowing what to do and not doing it. There were many times I yelled at my child and then felt remorseful because I knew better. Don't dwell on these feelings. Be gentle with yourself. Shake the feelings off and ask yourself what you would do differently next time. Just because you mess up doesn't mean you are back where you started. It doesn't mean you aren't making progress.

Some people feel awkward using authentic power (what authoritative parenting is made of) at first because it is new and, like stiff, new shoes, it feels cumbersome. If you had the task of pressing eighty-eight levers at prescribed intervals at a certain speed and, at any given time, you had to switch to a different set of levers using a different speed, could you do it? What I just described is the act of playing the piano. To play the piano well takes practice.

The same is true with these parenting techniques. They take practice and persistence. At first, you may feel uncomfortable, or you may find they don't work the way you expected. If you have been permissive, your child's behavior may even get worse when you start getting firmer. However, with patience and practice, you will become a more confident parent. Soon you'll be on the verge of doing something coercive and you'll catch yourself right before you do it. That's success!

### Concentrate on the Goal of Discipline

When a parent disciplines a child, the goal is to teach the child to be self-responsible and to act in ways that get positive results whether an authority figure is present or not. Discipline should increase children's awareness of their choices; these choices can make them happy or unhappy. Control over their behavior thus becomes internal and contributes to their self-esteem.

Children misbehave when they feel discouraged or powerless. When you use discipline methods that overpower or make them feel bad about themselves (autocratic parenting), you lower their self-esteem. It doesn't make sense to punish children who already feel bad about themselves by heaping on more discouragement.

When you do nothing or are ineffective in teaching the child new behavior skills, you likewise contribute to the child's feeling of discouragement and powerlessness (permissive parenting).

Authoritative parenting or an authentic use of power leads to meaningful relationships, synergy, calmness, tender moments, joy, and contentment. Parenting can be fun again!

# 5

# Live and Lead from Your Values— Your Child Is Watching

**J**ust as we often raise our children as we were raised by our parents, so we often live by the values our parents hold. Unless we consciously choose our values, most of us unconsciously accept our parents' values. It is also easy to succumb to the values of our social groups.

What exactly do we mean by "values"? Values are (1) the social principles, goals, or standards held or accepted by an individual, and (2) that which is desirable or worthy of esteem. Your values determine how you and your family live. A modest list of values you hold might include honesty, importance of family, having fun, being physically fit, maintaining a certain income, healthy eating, and being well educated. Your values may change. As your values change, your decisions and behavior change too, and bring you new experiences.

New experiences themselves can cause you to change your values. Perhaps someone close to you dies unexpectedly, and as a result you decide to let your loved ones know more frequently how much you love them.

It is important to evaluate your values. For example, you may value work more than you value time spent with your family. If this is the case, you may find that your children and your spouse are doing some negative things to get your attention. The atmosphere at home may feel tense or debilitating. You may feel sabotaged by your partner or feel like an outsider in your own family. However, let's say that instead of making work your highest priority, you decide to make your family your number one priority. As a result, you feel nourished and supported by your family.

One way you can determine what values you hold is to observe the quality of your life. If you don't feel nurtured within your family, look to see how much of yourself you're investing in them. What you spend time and money on can also reveal your values.

Reflecting on your values requires guts and honesty. For example, we might say we value the importance of living a healthy, stress-free life, but we continue to work at a very stressful job because we're afraid to quit and go without the level of income it provides. Perhaps we say it's important to us that our children don't watch too much television, but we allow them to watch because we need a "babysitter" while we do other things.

Actions speak louder than words, so examine how you live to find out what you truly value. If you don't like what you see, change your values and your behavior. You have the ability to design and create the family of your dreams.

Here is an exercise: Imagine for a moment that you are an architect and you have a family blueprint in front of you. Write down what your values are. What things do you hold dear that you don't want to waver on? What are things you want to improve? Some values might be family time, spiritual practices, time with your partner, eating healthy, environmental issues, social justice issues, resolving conflict peacefully, how you discipline, and so on. Prioritize your values.

Ask your coparent to do the same. I have found that writing the values separately helps you to stay true to your convictions and not be influenced by your partner.

Then, as a couple, come up with a list of ten values that you will strive for as a team. This task may cause some conflict. Your goal here is not to win or compromise but to reach an understanding. Whenever you're in conflict with someone, there is one factor that can make the difference between being damaging and deepening your relationship. This factor is your willingness to let go of your need to be right.

If you don't have a partner, get a friend or family member that you can give your list to and who can help support you in holding your values sacred.

These ten values then become your personal lighthouse that will guide you in your decision-making and your actions. You will then become a designer of your family and not a victim of it. This a process. It will take time. Check your progress throughout the year and celebrate your wins. Your values will change over time. So make sure you do this activity once a year.

Without defining your values, you let your lack of values define you. Unimportant things will dictate the way you live, and your goals and dreams will be much harder to achieve.

## Seven Ways to Teach Values

**1. Determine what values you want to live.** As your children become age appropriate, include them in making the list of family values by using consensus. This list will help you keep your attention on creating what you want your family to experience.

**2. Make agreements around your values.** Let your values guide what rules your family will live by. For example, if family time is important to you at dinner, don't allow interruptions such as phone calls or television. Require that everyone in the family be present, children and adults alike. If you value music, perhaps all the children take music lessons (let each child choose what instrument to play so that she or he will be inspired).

**3. Be unrelenting about observing your values.** Sometimes in an attempt to make life easier for ourselves, we let things slide. This habit causes situations to become more frustrating, and time must be spent putting life in order again. If you don't find time to be with your family, it's likely that your family will cease to value being a family. Members may drift apart, and it will be difficult to bring them back together. Start out in the manner you wish to go and stay with it.

**4. Reinforce your words with actions.** Talk to children about your actions. Tell them the good feeling that you acquire from acting on a value. For example, "I greeted people at church today. It really makes me happy when I can make people feel welcomed."

**5. Look for teaching opportunities.** Be alert for stories from real life, television, books, and newspapers that illustrate a value you think is important. For example, our son loves football. My husband got him a book about Emmitt Smith, a professional football player who lived by important values that our son could learn from. The author talks about the importance of holding on to a dream until it is realized, humility, the importance of leading a balanced life with work and family, and a good education.

Point out actions of neighbors and friends that demonstrate values. For example, I told my children about a friend who called me to apologize for lying to me the previous day. We discussed how much courage it took for her to call. I shared how much more I trusted her after her apology.

**6. Teach your child to prioritize.** Suppose your children value both friendships and good grades. When their friends call them while they're studying, they'll have to choose which of these values is more important at that moment. What questions could you ask to help them prioritize?

**7. Discuss your own struggles with your values.** Share with your children how you struggle with your values. For example, "My boss wants me to do something that would save the company money. I don't want to do it because it will hurt the environment. I'm really struggling with this because I'm not sure what he'll do if I stick up for what I believe." Hearing you think about values helps your children clarify their own values. It also helps them feel less alone in their struggles.

Be insistent, subtle, creative, and inviting about teaching values. Don't give boring lectures or stern orders, or use "bandwagon" approaches.

## *When Your Child Isn't Honoring a Value*

When children's behaviors aren't aligning with your family values, ask yourself the following questions to reason out why.

- Am I sending a clear message? For example, you may really want the television off three days a week, but you only occasionally ask your family to turn it off. You have not been specific about what you want.
- Are my actions congruent with my talk? A friend of mine was walking out of a store with his daughter when he noticed that the clerk had given him too much change. He headed back to the checkout counter as his daughter asked, "Why are you going back when she only gave you a dollar too much?" He replied, "My integrity is worth more than a dollar."
- Am I exerting too much control because I want my child to share my values? Sometimes children will get into power struggles over values if we're too pushy about them.

If your teenagers are rebelling against your values, it's not only normal but important for them to determine their own values. This is a stage, and they will grow out of it. They may not end up with all the same values you have, but most of them will be similar. This doesn't mean you diminish your values, but it may mean that you scrutinize which ones are worth pursuing. Remember that relationships trump rules every time.

I've found that having a blended family carries with it a host of difficult challenges—and opportunities for teaching values. Brianna was in her late teens when her father and I were planning a trip to see her gift sisters (stepsisters). I knew that if I tried to force her to go, it was likely she would balk.

So instead, I asked her if she knew what a circle of influence was. Upon her questioning, I explained my interpretation of Stephen Covey's well-known idea. There are three concentric circles of people or human influencers. The outside circle consists of acquaintances and society in general, and the second circle consists of friends, teachers, and coaches who go in and out of your life. The inner circle is the people who have the capacity to enhance your life in the long term, mostly family members. I continued by telling Brianna that these are the relationships you want to support and nurture. I asked her who she thought belonged in this circle. Her response was her father, her brother, and me. I concurred, and then prompted inquisitively, "What about Amy, Chloe, and Emily?" She thought for a moment and nodded her head in agreement.

Then I told her about the upcoming trip and asked if she wanted to come with us. She quickly responded yes. Had I made her come, she most likely would have sulked and been miserable the whole time we visited.

Without values, our children are left to their own devices or they pick up the values of their peers or the media. When you care enough to stick up for your values, your children develop a deep respect for you and themselves.

## Adventures Living with Values

To raise the awareness of values within your family, try this game:

1. Choose a different value at the beginning of each week. Write it on a piece of paper and tape it to the refrigerator where everyone can see it daily.
2. As a family, practice that value for a week by using it as a guide.
3. Get together at the end of the week or at your next family meeting and share your stories of the adventures you each had during the week of observing that value.
4. Decide if the value is one you wish to keep as a constant guide for behavior in your family. If it is, discuss other ways to observe it.
5. Pick a new value for the next week.

An example of how the game might work is this: A family picks responsible money management as the value. During the week, the parents develop a budget. One child makes a difficult decision about whether to buy a football or a skateboard. The teenager forgoes a shopping spree in favor of donating to the local food bank. The preschooler contributes his collection of pennies to buy guinea pig food. By the end of the week, the family will have other adventures to share revolving around money. Everyone in the family gets a chance to tell his or her story, and all listen respectfully.

# 6

# Keys to Effective Communication

One of the primary reasons communication is imperative is that it builds trust between you and your child. A key component of communication—listening—is also an indispensable one. If you wish to forge stronger relationships with your family members, don't just talk to them—listen intently to what they're saying. Good communication skills open up new opportunities to really get to know your child in ways that normal family life doesn't.

We also give our children an edge on their future success when we model these skills. Effective communication skills are given primary importance in the processes of selecting job and college applicants.

## Communicating Needs

Most misbehavior in adults and children is an attempt to communicate an unmet need. For example, I have noticed that I get irritable when I don't feel connected to my husband or my children.

Children are unaware of their needs and don't know how to communicate their needs at first. It shows up in their misbehavior. Some of the most common needs are to feel loved, be powerful, have a sense of belonging, and be heard, understood, and respected, to name a few.

Instead of being annoyed by misbehavior, get behind the unwanted behavior and find out what your children need. Then address the need.

> My son was seven when he first met Brian, who is now my husband. Tyler and I had been alone for about eighteen months. One day early in my relationship with Brian, we were driving in the car when Tyler started kicking the back of Brian's seat. I turned and asked him to please stop. He did—for about seven seconds. Then he started kicking again. I more firmly told him to stop. He did. The third time he started kicking, I asked, "Tyler, this isn't like you. [This was true; he was generally cooperative.] What do you need?" He thought for a moment and then told me that when Brian was around, he felt invisible. My heart melted.
>
> It dawned on me that his sense of belonging was being jeopardized by my being busy attending to this new and budding relationship. We immediately found ways to include him in our conversations, and his negative attention-getting behavior stopped.

Much conflict can be resolved quickly and smoothly by teaching your children how to communicate their needs and paying attention to others' needs. Problems occur in families and businesses when we don't know what we need and don't learn to communicate our needs effectively. Instead, we complain and blame others for our unhappiness.

## Honoring Feelings

What happened in your family when you expressed an emotion such as anger or sadness? Many of us were not allowed to express our big emotions when we were growing up. Some parents said things like, "Do you want something to cry about? I'll give you something to cry about!" Or "Go to your room and don't come out until you've calmed down!" The expression of intense emotion scared people.

Vulnerability was equated with weakness. Even the dictionary gives a negative definition of the word: "(1) capable of being physically or emotionally wounded or hurt (2) open to temptation, persuasion, censure, etc." (Collins English Dictionary). Who would want to admit to vulnerability with a definition like that? We need a new definition that features vulnerability as openness: the ability to express honestly how one feels.

In this society, we criticize or try to stop and/or get rid of things that we don't understand. Parents tell children they are wrong to feel as they do—"You shouldn't hate your sister," or "You should love Grandpa, even if he does say mean things to you—he's your grandpa."

Feelings are neither right nor wrong. They just are. Much of children's misbehavior can be successfully redirected by simply allowing full expression (in a safe and appropriate manner) of their feelings.

A feeling that is suppressed often escalates or goes underground only to rear its head later. Feelings that are allowed to be expressed dissipate.

## Feeling Stoppers

Feelings forced underground can cause misbehavior. Here is a list of "feeling stoppers," the actions parents take that cause children to stop expressing how they feel:

- Scolding
- Solving problems
- Moralizing
- Making fun of them
- Assuming the worst of them
- Denying
- Lecturing
- Giving unwanted advice
- Humiliating
- Being sarcastic
- Minimizing
- Imposing guilt
- Name-calling
- Punishing
- Pitying
- Rescuing
- Interrupting
- Helping too much
- Prying
- Shaming

We squelch our children's feelings when we deny their expression by making these sorts of comments:

- "How can you be hungry? You just ate."
- "Your mom/dad is only going to be gone for a few days, so there's no need to be sad."
- "Big boys/girls don't cry."

- "This won't hurt."
- "That's not what you really want to do."

Comments like these deny your children the right to feel what they feel. They teach children not to trust their judgment or intuition. What are they supposed to think, since they do feel what they feel? They are likely to be confused.

One reason we may repress our children's emotions is that we are uncomfortable with our own feelings. Parents who are in touch with their own feelings can respond in a more loving, accepting manner to their children when they express their feelings, including the "unpleasant" or intense ones.

Children try to protect themselves when parents use feeling stoppers. They think that it isn't safe to express who they really are, so they stuff their feelings—sometimes literally. One day, I watched a mother and her little boy, who was overweight, eating in a restaurant. The mother was incessantly nagging the boy. As she nagged, he stuffed food into his mouth as fast as he could. He seemed to be stuffing his feelings down with food.

Recent findings also suggest that if you don't express your feelings, the feelings stay within your body and contribute to disease. Children who feel dominated by their parents and unable to express their feelings may take their frustrations out on their younger siblings, pets, or other property. An emotion repressed persists. An emotion expressed dissipates.

## Feeling Encouragers

*Listening and understanding creates trust. Lecturing and telling creates division.*

—UNKNOWN

Children rarely leave our presence neutral. They will either leave engaged or unattached. The following "feeling encouragers" invite the expression of other people's feelings and leave them feeling engaged and connected:

• Listen intently. Sometimes this act alone is enough. When we listen, we are actually aiding other people in listening to themselves. It means *really* hearing what your child is saying, as well as what he or she may not be saying. It requires both hearing and seeing. Watch and listen to these four things:

1. Body posture
2. Facial expressions
3. Tone of voice
4. Attitude

• Ask questions that show you care. For example, ask, "How does that make you feel?"

• Affirm the feeling. This helps other people feel they are not alone in this feeling. "I can understand why you're angry."

• Repeat what you are hearing to help the child feel heard. "What I am hearing is that you are angry because your brother took your ball." Try not to put your agenda into this interpretation. For example, do not say, "What I am hearing is that you are angry because your brother took your ball after you called him a name."

• Validate your children. This helps them to not to feel wrong about how they feel. "If I were in your shoes, I would probably feel the same way."

• Explore with curiosity: "Tell me more."

• Allow emptying. If there is another emotion not expressed it is likely to pop up later in some unexpected form. Ask, "Is there anything else you would like me to know?" or "Did I get it all?"

• Encourage your children's thought process by saying something about what they are expressing: "You're really clear about what you want to have different."

• When appropriate, share a similar experience of your own to help your children feel that they are not alone: "When I was your age, I had trouble asking girls out too." Avoid hijacking your child's moment. Keep your story short to avoid lecturing.

• Ask questions to help your children solve the problem. Try not to give advice or solve the problem for them. Here are a few thought-provoking questions:

"That's a problem. How will you handle it?"

"What's one thing you could do to solve your problem?"

"What would _____ (your child's favorite hero) do?"

"What would you do if this happened again?"

"What could you do differently?"

Thinking of possibilities instead of dwelling on the problem gives one hope when things seem hopeless.

When a child expresses emotions, it's important that you first acknowledge, affirm, or empathize with her before you do any problem-solving. The feeling of being understood and accepted is crucial in helping children work through their emotions. If you rush your children into finding a solution before they feel understood, they are more apt to get frustrated or defensive. They may stop expressing themselves.

We tend to focus on behavior rather than children's feelings. And we get ourselves into deep trouble when we take the emotional outbursts personally rather than connecting through their emotional state.

I found myself in trouble when I noticed that I was not listening to my kids with the right intentions. I frequently listened so that I could fix any errors in their thinking. I wasn't listening with the intention of connecting.

Finding "your person," someone who totally gets you, is a gift beyond measure. Our kids want us to be that person.

## Six Ways We Subtly Communicate

1. **Tone of voice:** Is your tone critical or accepting and warm?
2. **Physical touch:** Are you using too much or too little for your child's comfort?
3. **Body language:** Is your body posture threatening, smothering, or closed? Or is it letting your child know you are available? Is it congruent with what you are saying?

4. **Facial expressions:** Are they communicating criticism, disappointment, or disinterest? Or are they engaged, inviting, and curious?
5. **Eye contact:** Are your eyes distracted or are they focused on your child?
6. **Timing:** Do you allow your child enough emotional space to process his or her emotions or your requests?

It takes using all your senses to fully be in relationship with your child to create security, safety, and connection.

## Holding Space

There is a powerful technique called *holding space* that can be used with anyone having a challenging emotion, whether that be anger, frustration, or grief. It is particularly helpful if your child or teen is throwing a tantrum. "Holding space" means being physically, mentally, and emotionally present for your children. It means putting your focus on your children to support them as they feel their feelings without adding your personal agenda.

To truly support children through their big emotions, we can't do it by taking their power away, shaming them, or overwhelming them with more information than they need. We must be prepared to step to the side so that they can make their own choices, offer them unconditional love and support, give gentle guidance when it's needed, and make them feel safe even when they are acting off kilter.

This method can be used with any human having a challenging emotion. Here are some steps:

1. Center yourself. Bring calm into the chaos.
2. Create a judgment-free zone.
3. Stay present. Do not numb out or zone out.
4. Listen intently with the sole intent to understand.
5. Say as few words as possible.

6. Don't jump in to solve or fix the problem.
7. Be open to whatever emotions arise.
8. Trust the person's process.
9. Resist the urge to rush the process or do or change anything.
10. Do not try to take away or soothe the person's pain.

For those of us who are problem solvers or don't like to see our loved ones in pain, this process can be very difficult yet freeing at the same time.

## Understanding Children of Divorce

Children have a right to be angry when their parents divorce. Probably the one thing that children want most in their lives is to have the two people they love live together and love each other. Allow your children to express their anger. Avoid feeling guilty or shameful about your divorce if you have been through one.

"Mom, I'm really angry you and Dad got a divorce!" said Chris.

"Yes, I can understand that, Chris. What is it about the divorce that makes you the angriest?" asked Mom.

Chris answered, "I don't like living in two houses. I don't know where my home is!"

"It's confusing to you to have two homes," Mom said empathetically.

"Yeah," he nodded.

"What else about the divorce makes you angry?" she asked.

"I don't like that we live so far apart," Chris shared. (The families lived in different states.)

"It would be great if we could jump in the car and see your dad!" said Mom, understanding her child's dilemma.

"Yeah!" exclaimed Chris.

"Is there anything else you would like to ask me or tell me?" asked Mom.

"Do you still love Daddy?" asked Chris.

"Yes. There is a part of me that still loves your daddy. I respect your dad a lot, but I don't want to be married to him," replied Mom truthfully. Satisfied with her answer, her son smiled and kissed Mom good night.

Notice how the mom invited her son to talk freely about the divorce. She offered no guilt, shame, blame, or excuses in the conversation.

Frequently, all we need to do is listen intently, hold the child, and be understanding. We get ourselves into a lot of trouble when we think we must heal, fix, rescue, or convert.

## Send "I" Messages

Sending an "I" message instead of a "you" message is not a new method of communication. However, I am reminding you of it because even though we might know about it, we may not be using it.

A child has taken his mom's jewelry to play with and doesn't put it back. Mom might say to her child, "Why do you always take my things? I can never find them. If you don't stop taking my things, I'm going to lock my door!" Her threat is out of proportion with the behavior. Most likely, the child will get defensive or tune her out. Mom could more effectively make her wishes about her jewelry known in the following manner:

> "I feel frustrated when you take my jewelry because when I want it, it isn't where I left it. I love your sense of style and I don't mind you playing with it. What I want is for you to put my jewelry back where you found it."

To communicate so that the other person is willing to listen, try this model:

"**I feel** [worried and angry]."

"**When** [you don't come home on time]."

"**Because** [I'm afraid you got hurt]."

"**What I want is** [for you to be on time, or call me if you'll be late]."

"**What I love about you is** [how much you enjoy your friends]."

> I was holding hands and roller-skating with my daughter. She said in a very demanding tone, "Skate faster!" This wasn't the first time I had noticed she was being demanding, so I said, "I don't feel like

cooperating with you when you use that tone of voice with me. If you continue, I'll skate by myself." Later, when she quit being demanding, I told her how much I loved skating with her.

When you communicate with your children, take responsibility for what you say and for what they hear. Watch facial expressions and body posture to make sure your children aren't discouraged by your communication. If your children start explaining themselves, defending themselves, rolling their eyes, getting quiet, or looking disgusted, they're probably feeling defensive. If this happens, focus on creating closeness first. Do something encouraging to create a more open atmosphere. Then express your feelings and desires in the manner shown above.

## Family Meetings

Living in proximity is challenging and requires some serious cooperation from everyone in a family. I recommend that you have family meetings once a week. Almost every corporation has meetings to help coordinate its activities. Our families are far more important than corporations and require a forum to communicate their functioning. Family meetings help children feel like they have a say in family decisions, and as a result, they feel more accountable to the family. These meetings can create an incredible feeling of support, promote bonding, and provide a forum for all the members to express their opinions in a safe place. To create that safety, it is essential that no criticism be allowed during these meetings.

Set aside a day of the week and a specific time to have your meetings. Make this time sacred. Do not make exceptions or changes to this time unless absolutely necessary. If you change meeting times at a whim, your family members may stop respecting them.

Family meetings are effective forums in which to discuss matters such as these:

- Coordination of everyone's schedule for the week
- Meal plans and who will prepare them

- Vacation plans
- Household chores and who will do what
- Conflicts between family members
- Personal issues for which someone wants help
- Encouragement
- Budgeting
- Announcements
- Family entertainment
- Everybody's goals for the week and how the family can support them to accomplish their goals

If a conflict occurs between siblings during the week, you can tell them to bring their grievance up at the family meeting. Stepping back from the conflict for a brief time gives everyone a chance to cool off. Postponement of a solution until the family meets also prevents the children from fighting for your attention.

Here are a few of the life skills your child can learn from family meetings:

- Budgeting
- Planning
- Leadership
- Followership
- Conflict resolution
- Self-control
- Giving and receiving encouragement
- Teamwork
- Time management
- Decision-making
- Prioritizing
- Time management
- Win/win negotiation

## Family Meeting Guidelines

Family meetings can be a very successful time in which you can solve problems as well as have fun. Here are some ideas for the format of a family meeting.

**Who and when.** Hold the meeting once a week at a time when everyone in the family can attend. Make an agreement that whoever can't attend (for an acceptable reason) will still abide by decisions made at the meeting. Even though your kids or your partner may usually be tethered to their phone, require that the phone be left in their room.

**Where.** Sit at a table—a round one if you have it so that everyone is equal—rather than lounging on couches and easy chairs. Do not have a meal at the same time or do other tasks.

**How.** Elect a new leader and secretary at every meeting so that everyone gets a turn. The leader calls on people to speak and sticks to the agenda; the secretary takes notes concerning what was discussed and decided. Later in the week, if there is disagreement about what was decided, the notes can be consulted.

• Begin the meeting with an encouragement feast for each family member. See the encouragement feast directions in the following box.

• Follow the agenda, which is developed over the week as family members add items to it (a blackboard or paper on the refrigerator is a good place to post it). Let the person who has the floor hold an object to signify that he or she is speaking. A stuffed toy or any special object works. If you aren't holding the object, you are listening, not talking. Teach your children that if they have a complaint, they need to have a suggestion for a solution. Tell them, "A person who is not part of the solution is part of the problem."

• Make decisions by family consensus, not by majority rule. That means everyone must agree. Sometimes it takes more than one family meeting to come to a decision. Aim for win-win decisions. Use the family meeting to practice this skill. Review the next week's calendar and plan family activities.

• Allow the leader to choose an enjoyable way to end the meeting. Some families like to have a snack or dessert, play a game or music together, or read a chapter in a book of interest to all. The goal is a pleasant activity that allows sharing. Make sure everyone feels good about the meeting, even when a decision gets postponed until the next meeting.

## Family Encouragement Feast

The family encouragement feast is an awesome way to lift everyone's spirits. An encouragement feast can be held at the dinner table, family meetings, in the car, or spontaneously anywhere, anytime. This is an exercise to focus on what you love about each other. At first, you may feel awkward if you're not accustomed to complimenting one another. That's OK. With practice, you will feel less self-conscious. The pleasure you see on the faces around you will keep you practicing.

Begin by putting a family member in the middle of a circle or at the head of the table, or in some other spot of honor. Choose the first person to be "it." Hold her or his hands (optional). Instruct each member of the family to say, "What I love about you is . . ." When each person has had a turn, the it person says what he or she loves about himself or herself and then chooses the next family member to be it. This continues until each person has had a turn. This game teaches your children the life skills of giving and receiving encouragement gracefully.

You can change the words to "What I appreciate," "What I respect," or any other word you would like to use to add some variety.

The closeness and warm, positive feelings make this the best family game ever!

Businesses and classrooms have even been known to use this process to start their meetings. It puts everyone in good spirits to begin their meeting or school day.

### How to Handle Difficult Issues

Don't let the meeting turn into a gripe session; if that happens, stop the meeting and do something to help the family feel close again. A great way to accomplish this is to have an encouragement feast. You want everyone to look forward to family meetings, and a gripe session is not the way to encourage repeat attendance.

If one of your children doesn't want to attend meetings, explore his or her reasoning and make the necessary amendments to ensure his or her presence.

During a family meeting, it's often necessary to address difficult issues or ask questions that may, at first, make children (and adults) feel defensive. It's essential that before doing this, you establish a trusting atmosphere. Once this friendly atmosphere is achieved, you can take a risk. Then, even if the children step back in caution from your approach, you can still maintain the necessary emotional closeness. However, if you confront them when the relationship is disturbed, your children may feel like their position is vulnerable. If they back off, you will have lost them.

> "Joe, can I talk to you a minute?" asks Dad.
>
> "What?" Joe responds in a gruff voice. [Caution: The relationship is disturbed. The parent must mend it before continuing.]
>
> "Sounds like you're expecting another lecture. Guess I do lecture you a lot, don't I?" Dad asks thoughtfully.
>
> "Ah, you aren't so bad," responds Joe.
>
> "Well, sometimes I catch myself treating you like you don't know anything, and that's not how I feel," admits Dad.
>
> "Don't worry about it, Dad. What did you want, anyway?" [Dad has now improved the relationship by talking about some of his own imperfections; it's now safe to approach Joe.]
>
> "Well, I wanted to see if we could work out a better way of keeping the family room clean. Do you have any ideas?" [If Dad had started directly with this question, Joe would have resisted finding a solution.]

With practice, you will find that you can interpret your child's response. This a vital tool when you are discussing and resolving relationship difficulties in the family meeting.

# 7

# Which Way to Responsibility?

Children who learn to be responsible for their actions and their own well-being have a great advantage in life. Helping them to understand and experience that responsibility gives you power and freedom. The responsible child gets to stay up later. The responsible teen gets to use the car more often. For children to be responsible, however, they need to know how to think creatively and to solve problems.

## Develop Their Internal Guidance System

Ideally, we want our children to do the right thing because it feels good inside. We don't want them to wait until the authority figure is out of sight and then do the wrong thing. When we punish, criticize, or shame children, we interfere with their ability to develop their own internal guidance system (IGS).

Here are some ways to foster a healthy IGS:

• Emphasize the joy of doing instead of outdoing.

• Ask questions that help children to self-reflect.

• Help your children focus on how they feel about things like their good grades, rather than praising them. Say, "It looks like you really like to learn" or "That must make you feel good." You want their good feeling to come from within.

• Stop praising them. If children feel they are OK only if they have someone else's approval, they develop the idea that other people's opinions are more important than their own and they may become a people pleaser. This character flaw can backfire when they become subject to peer pressure. People-pleasing can make them an easy target for inappropriate sexual activity, drugs, gangs, and physical abuse.

• Teach them to seek within instead of seeking without. Did you know that the average person gets bombarded with six to ten thousand advertisements a day? These ads urge you to have the next latest and greatest toy, accessory, and body. Following this path is like chasing the elusive snowflake. Once you have it, it melts away. True power and happiness come from within. We don't walk away empty-handed. Lorraine Murray, author of *Calm Kids: Help Children Relax with Mindful Activities*, suggests you can start teaching your child meditation as early as three years old!

## Teach Control over Their Emotions

You may want to read "The Tale of Two Wolves," an ancient Cherokee tale, to your children to help explain this concept. It goes as follows:

> There was a chill in the air as the children gathered around the campfire. A grandfather was telling them a story about the two wolves that lived inside them. The two wolves were doing battle with each other. One wolf was angry, jealous, competitive, and unhappy. The other wolf was loving, kind, generous, and joyful. As the grandfather paused, one of the children asked eagerly, "Grandfather, which one will win the battle?" The wise elder looked into the boy's wide eyes and answered, "The one you feed!"

Having the right attitude is a high commodity in most businesses today. Your children will be given an advantage when you teach them that emotions don't control us, but rather we control our emotions.

Tyler was furious with me for being late to pick him up from football practice. I apologized, empathized with him, and offered to do a make up. Tyler wouldn't have any of it and remained angry with me. I asked him, "It's OK to be angry with me. How long do you want to be mad?"

"Until dinner," he snapped.

I said, "That's a choice you have." He gave me the silent treatment for a few minutes and then changed the conversation to a happier note.

Teaching children that they control their emotions and not the other way around is integral to their happiness.

Attitudes are contagious. Bad moods can be passed on like a ripple effect, affecting numerous people throughout the day. Bad moods are like dark clouds that loom silently over your family, casting out connectivity and fun.

A method we used to counteract "the cloud" and teach our kids about emotions and how to have authority over them was to do a "heart check" with them several times a day. A "heart check" was their opportunity to check in with themselves to see how they were feeling and to change any negativity they were experiencing. At first, we asked them, "How does your heart feel?" and then moved on to just saying the words "heart check."

We particularly did this in the morning before school as we knew how important it was for them to arrive there with the most effective attitude for learning. Frequently a little coaching from us was required.

## Teach Self-Control

Self-control is one of the most important skills to teach your squirmy kids. It helps them manage impulses, emotions, and behaviors so that they can achieve long-term goals. It is a complex skill that develops over time. Some researchers say this skill is not fully developed until one's early twenties.

Developing self-control will in the long term help your children succeed academically and, later in life, financially. However, most important, it helps your child socially. Kids who are in control of their emotions and their actions fit in better with friends, and that will build their self-esteem.

In our instant gratification society, it is tricky to teach children self-control. Drive-through windows, high-speed Internet, and Alexa provide fast fixes to many of our desires. Because we appreciate these niceties, teaching self-control requires some creativity and ingenuity.

> A vacationing family sat next to me on the plane. The four-year-old started whining loudly, "I want to sit next to you, Daddy!"
>
> Dad responded, "On the next flight you can sit next to me." Throughout the ninety-five-minute flight, the little boy continued begging but Dad held his ground despite the glaring eyes of his fellow travelers. Dad calmly and lovingly said each time, "Next flight, buddy."

Delayed gratification can be taught when you have your children wait in line, sit still in restaurants, and take turns in playing games. As your children get older, gardening, baking, and having them earn money for something they want are a few of the things that enhance this skill. Keep your intention on the value of teaching self-control and you will be surprised at how creative you can be.

## Teach Your Child How to Make Decisions

Helping your children make good decisions can make their lives a lot easier. This skill is based on considering alternatives. In the short run, it's easier for parents to make decisions for their children. What is appropriate decision-making on behalf of a two-year-old becomes inappropriate decision-making for a five-year-old, and so on as the child grows. Recall that you are gradually working yourself out of the job of parenting.

> A four-year-old was screaming because she didn't want to go to bed. This was after her father went through their bedtime routine and had met her needs. Her dad came to the door and said, "If you want to continue screaming, I will close the door. If you decide to be quiet, I

will leave it open." The little girl thought for a moment and then sat down and began to look at a book quietly. Her dad left the door open and went back to his activity.

A woman's seven-year-old nephew asked, "Do you think it would be all right if I brought these candies with me to the funeral?"

His aunt replied, "Think about the situation. We are going to the funeral home, which is a very quiet place to say goodbye and be respectful. When you decide what you want to do, let me know."

The boy pondered his dilemma for a few moments and then told his aunt that he had decided not to bring the candies with him.

A teenager asked his mom at 9:00 PM if he could go to his friend's house. Her first urge was to say, "No, you haven't done your homework, and it's late." Instead, she bit her tongue and said, "Think about how much time you need to do your homework and how much time you need for sleep, then decide." Her son decided to go to his friend's house for fifteen minutes. Mom knew that if she had told her son what to do, he would have rebelled and gone off for half the night. Given the opportunity, he made a responsible decision.

In each situation above, the adults expected the children to think and make reasonable decisions. The teenager appropriately had a more complex situation to think about than the boy or the preschooler. It would have been easy for the adults to tell the children what to do. Instead, each child was given time to think and allowed to make his or her decision.

Questions to ask your child to emphasize this skill are:

- "You have a decision to make here. How will you make it?"
- "How did you come up with that decision?"
- "What was the result of your decision?"
- "If you could make a different decision, what would you decide?"
- "What information do you need to make a good decision?"

## *Trust Your Child*

One thing I appreciated about my parents was that when I became a teenager, they didn't tell me what time to be home, but would ask me, "What time will you be home?" They trusted me and respected my ability to make a responsible decision. As a result, I made a conscious effort to live up to that trust. I came home when I said I would because we shared mutual respect, not because I was afraid of what they might do or say to me.

# Teach Your Children to Trust Their Intuition

One way you can help your children make decisions is by helping them trust their intuition about what is right. When your children ask you what to do, instead of telling them, ask them to quiet their minds and get their answer from inside themselves. If the answer they get is based on fear, tell them to look again for a different answer. Encourage your children to think in this manner:

> Alicia approaches her mother, crying, "Blaire doesn't want to play with me anymore."
>
> After some discussion about how Alicia feels, Mom asks, "What will you do?"
>
> Alicia says, "I don't know."
>
> Mom suggests, "Why don't you get really quiet and ask yourself what the best thing to do would be."
>
> Several minutes later Alicia returns to tell Mom that she has decided that she isn't going to play with Blaire anymore. Mom observes that this decision is probably based on fear and suggests that Alicia try the quiet method again.
>
> This time Alicia returns happier, yet more determined. "I decided to call Blaire to see if she's still mad at me," she reports.
>
> Mom says encouragingly, "That's brave of you."

The reality of what you say must correspond to the child's intuitive sense of what is true and real. To act on their intuition, children need to believe that their perceptions are accurate. One day my son asked, "Mommy, why are you mad?"

Caught off guard, I said, "I'm not mad." Then I realized I had been mentally reviewing a conflict with someone from earlier in the day. My son's intuition was correct. "You're right, I was angry about something that happened at work. Thanks for helping me recognize that," I told him.

Children are very sensitive to the "vibes" around them. When we lie or deny an emotion, we teach them to doubt their intuition. Sometimes we lie to protect children—or so we think. They usually know when something is wrong, and their imaginations can create a situation worse than the real one. At the very least, we cause great confusion. Confusion gets in the way of good decision-making.

## Teach Conflict Resolution

Some degree of conflict is always inevitable in every close relationship. Conflict can be viewed as bad and something to be avoided. However, conflicts are integral to our growth.

Here are some reasons why conflict is important.

1. Conflict is healthy for relationships because it signals a need for change, for both parties. Conflict provides an opportunity for making changes, if both partners are up for it.
2. Conflict makes you grow. It forces you to get to know and understand yourself and your family members better.
3. If done effectively, conflict draws you together as a team by forcing you to problem-solve together.

## Steps for Conflict Resolution

As often as possible, solve problems using a win-win format. Your child will feel esteemed and be more cooperative, and so will you. The brainstorming process that is part of negotiation may seem tedious and cumbersome at first. With practice, you will find that it comes more easily, with efficient and rewarding results. Here is an example of how it works:

**Problem:** Three-year-old Ivan comes into Mom's bed during the night. Mom is frustrated that he disturbs her sleep.

**Step 1.** Ask permission to work on the problem with the other person. "Ivan, is this a good time to do some brainstorming?" Getting permission shows respect for the other person's time. Your child or partner may not be in the mood, or they may be preoccupied with something.

**Step 2.** Tell your child what you want and why you want it clearly, simply, without guilt, blame, shame, or exaggeration. Use "I" statements (see page 87). "It wakes me up when I get kicked in the middle of the night. I wake up and I can't get back to sleep. I want you to sleep in your own bed."

**Step 3.** Ask your child to share how he or she feels and what he or she wants (gather information, making sure your child feels heard and understood). You need to know so that you can arrive at a solution that allows both of you to win. "I get lonely in my bed all by myself. I want to sleep with someone," says Ivan.

**Step 4.** Make a list on paper of the possible solutions to the problem. Be creative, and don't judge a solution at this point. Sometimes it helps the process to put down things you think are crazy, just to loosen up. You often create the best solutions when you are fun and lighthearted. The important rule of brainstorming is that you don't criticize or reject any idea at this listing stage. Anything goes! If your brainstorming partner is critical and won't become positive, stop the process and wait until later to try again.

**Step 5.** When you've thought up all the ideas you can, give the list to your child first. Have him or her cross out any idea he or she doesn't like, then take the list and cross out the ideas you don't like. You can read the list to children who can't read by themselves and help them cross off ideas.

**Step 6.** Pick one idea or a combination of ideas from those remaining on the list to be the solution. In the spirit of win-win, make sure you are both satisfied. Read your child's body language and tone of voice to make sure he or she really is happy with the solution. If he or she says OK but doesn't mean it, the solution won't work. In that case, choose a different solution.

**Step 7.** Use the solution for a specified time. If that solution doesn't work, brainstorm again for a new one. Don't give up, and keep a positive attitude.

Here is the list Mom and Ivan made:

- Mom could let Ivan sleep in her bed.
- Ivan could stay in his bed.
- Ivan could sleep in Mom's bed twice a week.
- Mom could sleep in Ivan's bed in his room.
- Ivan could sleep in his sleeping bag on the floor next to Mom's bed.
- Ivan could sleep with his stuffed animal.
- They could all sleep on the couch in the family room.
- Ivan could sleep with his cat.
- Mom could have another baby who could sleep in Ivan's room.

Mom and Ivan decided that Ivan could sleep in a sleeping bag on the floor in Mom's room for as long as he wanted to. Both Mom and Ivan were happy with this solution. Ivan slept in the sleeping bag for approximately three months and then stayed in his room.

The win-win problem-solving works with teenagers as well.

**Problem:** Mom and fifteen-year-old Tamara agreed to work on a problem Mom had. Tamara was often late getting home in the evening. Mom didn't want to worry about her.

The two of them came up with these ideas in their brainstorming session:

- Tamara could go without a curfew.
- Mom could tell her that if she wasn't home by 11:00 PM, she had to come home at 10:00 PM the next night she was out.
- Tamara could wake Mom up when she got home so Mom wouldn't worry.
- Mom could set an alarm, and if Tamara wasn't home when it went off, Mom would call her and/or her friends.

Mom and Tamara decided that Mom would set an alarm for 11:15 PM. If Tamara got home by 11:00 PM, she would turn it off. If the alarm went off, then Mom would start calling Tamara or her friends if needed.

## Let Your Child Be Bored

How many times have you heard the words "I'm bored"? You may think, "With all the new-fangled toys he has, how can he be bored?" This phrase seems to be heard more frequently since video games were invented. The reason is that video games provide releases of dopamine, a feel-good chemical, every few minutes. It is easy for your child to get addicted to these chemical rushes. Regular life, sadly for some children, seems boring compared to it.

Don't be afraid to let kiddos be bored. Studies have shown that operating under the notion that boredom leads to kids' getting in trouble and should be constantly scheduled can have a detrimental effect on their imagination.

It is not your job to make your children happy. If you keep filling up their time, you will interfere with their learning the life skill of self-discovery. Boredom can spur your children to engage in activities that they normally would not have experienced such as photography, cooking, doing a DIY project, or fixing a bike.

Allowing boredom results in your children's having more time and freedom to explore their own interests, their own identity. In addition, it pushes them to find a deeper meaning in life. For example, the child who explores the woods next door develops a deeper connection to nature.

When your children say they're bored, reply with, "Oh, what will you do?" instead of providing an array of choices of things for them to do. If they ask for suggestions in an appropriate tone of voice (without whining, pouting, or looking sad), then you may want to give an occasional suggestion, but avoid making the arrangements. Let them take responsibility. If their tone is inappropriate, you may want to leave the room or ignore the request until they ask pleasantly. If they beg to play video games outside the agreed-on time limits, say, "Not an option," and walk away. Do not argue with your children.

At a fun time (not when your children are complaining about not having anything to do), brainstorm a list of things they might enjoy, such as photography, painting, making dinner, planning the next family outing, or researching something of interest. *Do not* add your agenda to the list, tempting as it may seem. Put the lists on their doors. Or put the items on a sheet of paper, cut them out, and put them in jar. The next time they are bored, have them draw a slip of paper from the jar or check out the list on the back of the door.

The next time you hear those words, instead of getting frustrated with your children, see their boredom as an internal push to seek out something new. Holding this thought will help keep you from becoming irritated.

## Teach Your Children That Happiness Is an Inside Job

It's your children's job to learn how to make themselves happy. When we entertain our children, take care of all their needs, smooth over the troubles, and provide material goods for their comfort and plea-sure, we allow them to develop an attitude that others should make life exciting and comfortable for them. Children pout and whine and parents go into action trying to make their children happy.

Instead, parents would be wise to teach their children that hap-piness is not dependent on others or external circumstances. Their happiness is their responsibility.

> Dexter was sad about not being invited to a birthday party. Mom observed her son moping around the house. Mom inquired about his sadness and after empathizing she asked, "How long do you want to *choose* to be sad?"

The word *choose* is emphasized here because children need to learn that they are not the victims of their emotions. Rather, they are in control of their emotions. Another powerful phrase to mem-orize for further use is, "What is one thing you could you do to make yourself feel better?" This question puts children in charge of their feelings.

### *How to Get the Love They Want*

Teach your children how to take responsibility for getting the love they want. We can't expect other people to read our minds and know when we need outward expressions of love and affection. One way to teach this is to model for your children the kind of love you want. For example, "It really makes me feel loved when you play with my hair" or "I love it when you rub my feet."

Be sure to ask them what makes them feel loved. It might be fun to read Gary Chapman's book *The 5 Love Languages* with your family to help determine each other's love language. Another way for your children to develop this skill is to have family "love bags." Each family member has a separate bag. In each bag, the children put small strips of paper on which they have written something that would help them feel loved. For example, "Read me a book, please," "Rub my feet, please," "Tell me something you love about me, please," "Listen to me for fifteen minutes, please," and so forth.

Make sure the request can be fulfilled at the time it's made and requires nothing more than time and attention. Requests to buy things are not suitable for the love bag. You don't want your children to associate being loved with money or things. When your children feel discouraged or unloved, they can take their love bag to a willing family member to draw from it and fulfill their request.

This is also a great way to circumvent discipline problems. Instead of misbehaving to get your attention, your children can bring you their love bag and get love in an appropriate way.

Love bags work for every family member. You and your spouse may want to have a separate, private love bag for yourselves! It's never too late to take responsibility for your own happiness.

## Teach Your Children to Give Their Personal Best

Emphasize *personal* best rather than a comparison to someone else's achievement. Ask, "Did you do your best?" instead of, "Were you the best?" When you do not compare your children to someone else, they are more likely to enjoy doing their best. If they know how to recognize their own effort, they won't be so discouraged when someone else is better than they are. There will always be someone better, so it's good to learn early in life that comparisons generally lead to a feeling of arrogance or defeat.

Some children are capable of looking at another person's accomplishment and see areas and ways to improve. This is a legitimate observation provided it doesn't lead to the child's giving up.

### Go the Extra Mile

We're so thankful when our children actually complete the task we asked them to do that we forget to teach them the value of going the extra mile. You know what a great feeling it is when you put forth that extra effort, even if no one else notices. Teach your children this by acknowledging their efforts, starting when they are toddlers. In time, they will internalize your encouragement. They will feel pride when they put flowers on the table or fold the napkins a special way or recheck their homework even when they weren't asked.

## Encourage Altruistic Behavior

Provide your child opportunities to give without expecting something in return. Children need to feel good about themselves, and helping others can provide these good feelings. Volunteering to pick up community trash, working at a pet rescue facility, or visiting the elderly are just a few things that can encourage altruism. An offer of money can dampen the experience for the child. If you wish to encourage altruism, make sure you don't confuse your child with material reward.

## Expect Your Children to Be Capable

We often do things for our children because we can do them more quickly and efficiently. We are, however, robbing children of the chance to learn by experience and to build self-confidence. When you act as if your children can handle a situation, they sense that you have confidence in them. They will feel encouraged to do things beyond what they think are currently possible.

Be particularly wary about doing something for children who say "I can't" when you've already seen that they can. Let them practice and gain more confidence in their abilities.

> Nate is trying to tie his shoes. "Mommy, I can't!" he wails.
>
> Mother, who is not in a hurry, says in a friendly voice, "I think you can handle it." She smiles at Nate and leaves the room.

Mother's tone of voice was very accepting. She wasn't annoyed with Nate. She was telling him that she had confidence in him, both with her words and her actions. If you leave the room, you will find it easier to keep from coaxing, becoming annoyed, or doing the task for your child. Give your child the benefit of the doubt. You may be surprised!

## Ask for Your Children's Help

Children sometimes feel like dwarves in a world of competent giants. They overestimate how much parents can do (some younger children feel as though parents are perfect) and underestimate their own worth. A very effective way to build children's self-confidence is to ask for their help. Do you remember how important and worthwhile you felt when a respected friend has asked you for your help? Give your children the chance to feel that way too. My young son's fresh viewpoint really helped me one day:

> I came home upset about a conflict I'd had with one of my employees. Five-year-old Tyler could see that I was unhappy and asked me, "What's that face, Mommy?" I told him the situation and asked him if he had any suggestions about what I should do. He thought for a moment. Valentine's Day had just passed, and he suggested that I give my coworker one of his Valentine cards. At first I shrugged off the idea in my head, thinking how silly it would be to do that. Then I thought, *Why not?*

Tyler helped me find an unused Valentine. The next day I gave it to my employee, saying, "I felt so bad about what happened between us yesterday that I asked my son what I should do. Tyler suggested that I give you this Valentine." She started to cry, I started to cry, and we resolved the conflict right then and there. That night, I shared with Tyler what had happened and thanked him for helping me solve my problem. Imagine how proud he felt of himself for being able to help his grown-up mom solve one of her work problems!

Here is an example of how one father's kids helped him in a crisis:

Shortly before the camp I ran was to begin, I received a call from a father who had enrolled his two sons. He told me that he had suffered a major financial crisis in his business, and he was unable to send his boys to camp. He wanted some suggestions on how he could break the bad news to his boys. I suggested that, rather than tell the boys he couldn't afford to send them to camp, he ask for their help in deciding how to handle the crisis.

Several evenings later he phoned and told me, "I said to my sons, 'Boys, I've made a mistake in my business and lost a big order. Because of this, we're going to be very short on money for a while. Do you guys have any ideas that might help me solve this problem?' The boys' response was amazing. They volunteered to give up camp. They also offered to start turning off unnecessary lights and to get paper routes.

"But the greatest benefit is that their eagerness to help has made the whole problem less of a threat to me. I feel like I have the support of my family. I made a huge mistake, yet our family is closer than ever!"

This father's willingness to be vulnerable and to ask for the children's help avoided a possible family crisis and made him feel accepted even though he was at fault. He gave his children the opportunity to help and to feel like their ideas made a difference, and perhaps most important, he showed them that admitting a mistake is a responsible thing to do.

## Teach Children Money Management

Money management is an essential skill that every child needs to know in order to be responsible. Schools do not teach this skill. They may teach children how to count coins, but they don't teach smart ways to manage money.

I never heard my parents talk about money. Some kids hear about money only when their parents fight about it. You will be giving your kids a financial edge by teaching budgeting, saving, investing, and how to prosper from compound interest. Buy them a stock and let them watch it grow.

To teach my children about money, I gave them a weekly allowance for being a member of the family that was not tied to whether they did their chores. They had chores, and then they had extra chores that they could do to earn money. They were expected to pay for half of any toy they wanted. And as they grew older, they were given a monthly allowance to budget for things like clothes and entertainment.

One of my biggest mistakes that I hope you can learn from is lending my child money with his promise to pay me back when we got home from a shopping adventure. I very seldom required that he pay me back. This disservice materialized later in his life when he had trouble managing money the first few years of his adult life.

Even if your family doesn't need extra money, have your child get a job. Start early with pet sitting, babysitting, lawn mowing, and so on. Parents are often afraid to let their kids get a job because they don't want a job to interfere with their academics. Experience is often our best teacher.

## Remind Your Children That They Make a Difference

Children, especially teenagers, feel like they are treated like "just a kid" and don't really make a difference in the world. They tend to feel that the adults have all the authority and that what they think, feel, and do doesn't really matter. Remind your children frequently that they do make a difference. Tell them when their suggestions or efforts help you or someone else. For example, you might say, "You know, that advice you gave me about your little sister was very helpful. I tried what you suggested, about not giving in to her, and it really worked."

To give them ideas, watch shows together about what kids do to make a difference. Take, for example, Greta Thunberg, the Swedish environmental activist who is known globally for challenging world leaders to take action on climate change mitigation. She has won numerous awards including *Time* magazine's Person of the Year. She started her efforts when she was fifteen, outside the Swedish parliament.

Teens especially need to feel hopeful and have a sense of purpose to help them navigate this tumultuous stage of life.

## Hand Over Responsibilities

Don't give your kids only responsibilities that relate to their personal effects, such as picking up their belongings, making their bed, and cleaning their room. One of the best ways you can teach your children responsibility is to provide many opportunities for them to contribute to the family. Avoid giving them only the "low-dignity jobs," such as taking out the garbage and cleaning up the dog's messes. Include tasks that get more recognition, such as helping to create the family budget, shopping, or cooking a meal. Let them know how important their contribution is.

Children learn responsibility by being responsible for tasks appropriate to their age. I could stand and watch an expert hit tennis balls forever, but unless I'm given the opportunity to experience the results of my mistakes and the joy of my successes with that ball and racket, it's unlikely that I'll develop my tennis skills by simply observing. Likewise, children will never learn to get themselves out of bed on time if their parents take the responsibility away from them by waking them every day. They need to feel the consequences of oversleeping and the pride of self-reliance when they get up on time.

Be sure to give responsibility in an empowering way. For example, instead of saying, "It's about time you started doing your own laundry," say, "I've noticed that you are handling responsibility for picking up after yourself really well. I think you're ready to learn how to do your own laundry."

Teach the skills that are needed and supervise carefully if needed for safety. The following list is by no means exhaustive, but it serves as a guide for parents who don't realize how much their children are capable of at an early age.

Each month, ask yourself, "What am I doing for my children this month that they may be ready to take responsibility for doing on their own?" Maybe a preschooler is now capable of making his or her own bed in the morning, or an older child is now ready to do his or her own laundry, or a teenager can make his or her own dental appointments. Make sure you turn over responsibilities you know they can handle.

These gradual gifts of responsibility will prove to be far less overwhelming to your children than if you wait until they are sixteen, eighteen, or twenty-one and suddenly declare, "You're an adult now—handle your own laundry." If you implement this plan, you'll be amazed to see how much responsibility children can learn to manage and enjoy at even a young age.

# Tasks Children Can Do to Learn Responsibility

| 18 months to 3 years old | 4 to 6 years old | 7 to 10 years old | 11 to 15 years old | 16 to 18 years old |
|---|---|---|---|---|
| Turn off lights while being carried | *All the previous, plus:* | *All the previous, plus:* | *All the previous, plus:* | *All the previous, plus:* |
| Carry in the newspaper or mail | Help find grocery items in the store | Get up on time in the morning | Babysit | Run errands |
| Get cereal or snack from kid-friendly containers | Help fold towels and washcloths | Help wash and vacuum car | Cook meals | Balance family checkbook |
| Wash tables and counters with damp sponge | Pour things | Wash dishes | Buy groceries from a list | Handle own checking account |
| Pick up toys and clothes | Give you a back rub or foot rub | Fix snacks and light meals | Wash windows | Maintain car |
| Put soiled or wet diaper in the diaper pail | Help measure ingredients | Help read recipes | Change light bulbs | Help with family budgets |
| Wash vegetables, tear lettuce, stir | Count goods at the grocery store | Run washing machine and dryer | Make appointments | Take care of house/garden/yard chores |
| Help set the table | Water plants | Change sheets on the bed | Order takeout food for family | Take care of animals |
| Feed and water pets | Sort white clothes from dark clothes for laundry | Help with projects around house | Wax car | Help younger children with homework |
| Help clean up after meals and play | Help with vacuuming, sweeping, and dusting | Read to younger siblings | Mow lawn | Take care of siblings |
| Wake up sibling | Gather library books to return | | Operate saws for home projects | Work outside the home |
| Run simple errands around the house | Help younger siblings | | Help in parent's business | |
| Carry in light groceries | Help plant a garden | | | |
| Help put groceries away | Wash the floor | | | |
| Scramble eggs, make toast with supervision | Put dishes in dishwasher | | | |
| Help make beds | Measure soap for dishwasher and start cycle | | | |
| Put plastic dishes in the dishwasher | Be responsible for compost buckets | | | |
| Make salads | Haul things in a wagon | | | |
| Bring recyclables to the recycle bins | Assist in meal planning | | | |
| Lead family prayers | Make a simple meal | | | |
| Put own clothes away | Empty dishwasher and stack dishes on counter | | | |
| Take clothes out of the dryer | Rake leaves for short periods of time | | | |
| Tell you when the traffic light turns green | Help wash pets | | | |
| Clear dishes from the table | Prepare own lunch | | | |
| | Walk well-behaved pets | | | |
| | Carry in firewood | | | |
| | Start to manage own money | | | |

# 8

# Your Child Is Not Misbehaving

**C**hildren usually misbehave because they are fulfilling a need. Your children are communicating with you about their needs when they misbehave. To teach your children a better way to tell you what they need, you must figure out what goals they have in mind. Identify your children's goals before you decide how to discipline them. This is easier to do than you may think.

It is important to understand why your children behave as they do, so that your response is the effective one. For example, if you view a toddler who tries to flush a roll of toilet paper down the toilet as "bad," you have failed to recognize the toddler's need to experiment. Toddlers learn how the toilet works by exploring, and until they try to flush the roll and see the result, they will not understand why they can't flush something so large. If, on the other hand, you view the experiment for what it is, you can show them what they can flush safely.

Your job as a parent is to meet your children's needs appropriately. In the process, they will be learning how to meet their own needs as they grow.

## Importance of the Correct Diagnosis

Three people visited the doctor for three different reasons.

Doctor: "What seems to be your problem?"

Patient 1: "I have a headache."

Patient 2: "My foot hurts a lot."

Patient 3: "My arm hurts whenever it's cold outside."

Doctor: "I can help you all! Since none of you feel good, I'll take out your gallbladders. Why, just six months ago I had a patient who didn't feel good. I took out his gallbladder, and now he feels fine!"

Would you trust a doctor who thinks like this? Of course not: (a) he didn't take the time to make a proper diagnosis, (b) he assumed everyone's problem was the same, (c) he believed one solution would work for every problem. The necessity for correct diagnosis is obvious in the medical field. We sometimes overlook its importance in parenting.

Unfortunately, no one discipline method will be effective in every situation. To determine what method to use, you must take time to think about why your children are behaving the way they are. Until you understand the goals of your children's misbehavior, you can't be sure which action will be most effective. Rudolf Dreikurs, MD, author of *Children: The Challenge*, categorizes misbehavior into four goals: attention, power, revenge, and avoidance. Parents must identify these goals and take the right steps to redirect their child.

# MISTAKEN GOAL CHART

©INCAF By Kathryn Kvols

| If you feel: | And if your child has this reaction to a reprimand: | And your child's actions seem to be saying: | Then, this goal is most likely to be: | Corrective measure | Teach your child to: |
|---|---|---|---|---|---|
| •Annoyed <br>•You want to remind or coax <br>•Delighted with your "good" child | •Temporarily stops disturbing action when given attention | •"I only count when I am being noticed or being served." | **Attention** | Do all of the following as soon as the child begins to annoy: <br>•No eye contact <br>•No words <br>•Nonverbally make the child feel loved | •Ask for attention appropriately |
| •Provoked <br>•Challenged <br>•The need to prove your power <br>•"I'll make you do it!" <br>•You can't get away with this | •Intensifies the actions <br>•Wants to win <br>•Wants to be the boss | •"I only count when I am dominating or you do what I want or when I prove that you can't boss me." | **Power** | •Give choices, not orders <br>•Don't argue <br>•Use friendly eye contact <br>•Be firm and calm <br>•Give the child useful ways to feel powerful | •Win-win negotiate <br>•Be a leader |
| •Hurt <br>•Angry <br>•How could you do this to me? | •Wants to get even <br>•Makes self unlikable | •"I want to hurt others as I feel hurt." | **Revenge** | •Empathize <br>•Do not hurt back <br>•Reestablish the relationship <br>•Make amends <br>•Use logical consequences that are not punishing | •Assert feelings of hurt in appropriate ways <br>•Take responsibility for the results of his or her behavior |
| •Despair <br>•What can I do? <br>•Annoyed and/or pity | •Feels there is no use to try <br>•Passive <br>•Withdrawn | •"I can't do anything right so I won't do anything at all." <br>•"I'm no good." | **Avoidance** | •Don't coax or show pity <br>•Arrange small successes <br>•Avoid doing for the child <br>•Find situations for child to feel valuable <br>•Redirect their self-talk | •Accomplish and overcome <br>•Feel capable and worthwhile |

# 9

# Redirecting the Mistaken Goal of Attention

**The way parents respond to their children** is very important. Children base future behavior on their parents' reactions to what they do. Here is a perceptive child who gets attention for negative behavior because she couldn't succeed in getting it any other way.

Twenty-month-old Mariana sat quietly rocking in her rocking chair as her father worked on his computer. She began to rock faster and faster until the chair tipped over, spilling her to the floor with the chair on top of her. Immediately, her father jumped up, ran over, picked up the chair, and rescued his daughter. He carried her in his arms to his chair and spent fifteen minutes comforting her on his lap.

About three days later, Mariana approached her father, who again was on his computer. She tried climbing onto his lap, but he was being uncooperative. He gently brushed her aside, saying, "Not now, honey." The little girl walked over to the rocking chair, looked back at her father who was still absorbed in his computer, and tipped the chair forward until its back rested on the floor. Quietly, she squirmed under the chair and started crying. Success! Dad rushed to pick her up and consoled her in his lap again.

Children need and are entitled to our attention so their brains can develop in a healthy way. They know this instinctively and often interpret negative attention as better than no attention at all.

> Mother and her best friend are visiting over coffee. Four-year-old Isaac runs into the room and stands behind the sofa. In a whiny voice, he asks, "Mom, where's my airplane?"
>
> Mom stops talking to her friend and says, "I'm busy now. It's in your room." She resumes talking to her friend.
>
> Isaac interrupts again, "Where in my room?"
>
> This time Mom interrupts her friend and says, "In your toy chest. . . . I'm sorry, what were you saying?" Mom turns her attention back to her friend.
>
> Isaac persists, "Would you help me find it?"
>
> Mother jumps from the sofa in exasperation, "Oh, all right! But when I find it, I want you to play with it in your room so I can talk to my friend."

Isaac's request for help sounds innocent enough, right? However, the clue that it isn't lies in mother's feeling of exasperation. What would be a more acceptable way for Isaac to behave while his mother talks with her friend? He could respect her statement that she's busy and leave her alone. He could find the toy himself or play with something else. What does he really want from his mother? He wants to be the center of her attention; he may be wondering if she loves him if she isn't paying attention to him.

In this example, Issacs's inappropriate demands for attention were made in a relatively positive way. When children are more discouraged, their demands for attention may be more negative. For example, children might start playing with something they're not allowed to play with or pick a fight with their brother or sister. Some other ways of getting attention are whining, dawdling, forgetting, acting helpless, interrupting, or repeating an annoying behavior.

> A mom and dad were trying to have a conversation on an airplane. In the middle of their conversation, they allowed their four-year-old to

interrupt numerous times by persistently whining until she got attention from one of them. This child didn't learn about developing patience, respect for others, or self-control. These parents could do well by adopting the Montessori method (one of my favorite forms of education) of teaching children how to get their needs for attention met appropriately and respectfully. Children put their hand on the teacher's arm to indicate their need. The teacher acknowledges the child's request by putting his or her hand on top of the child's hand. This notifies the child that the teacher is aware of the child's presence. The child waits patiently until the teacher turns his or her attention to the child.

Remember that it is OK for a child to want attention; it's a legitimate human need and is shared by all children and adults. What we are addressing is the child's inappropriate ways of trying to get attention.

The way you can identify the goal of attention is by the way you feel and by how you would usually respond to the child's behavior. For the child whose mistaken goal is attention, you will feel frustrated and annoyed. You tend to respond by giving negative attention. Not all children use negative behavior to get attention, however. Consider the children who are being especially good to get attention. It is important for them to be good and to please you. These children are often called a "goody-goody" at home and a "teacher's pet" at school. Again, your response to your children's behavior is the important clue. When you feel annoyed by their striving to please you or be good, it is an indication that their mistaken goal is attention.

Here are four steps to redirect the goal of attention:

**1. Make no eye contact with children who are misbehaving.**

**2. Do not talk to them.** This step, as well as step 1, describe how to ignore children when they are trying to get your attention inappropriately. Ignoring is not enough, however. If you only ignore, your children's behavior is likely to escalate.

**3. Do something physical to make them feel loved.** The best way to do this is to touch them lovingly by rubbing their back, stroking their hair, or with some other physical gesture of love that they prefer. Don't pat their head because this is demeaning.

**4. Take action immediately.** Do the first three steps—no eye contact, no words, and physical touch to help the child feel loved—as soon as you start feeling annoyed. Do not wait. If you wait, you'll get angry, which makes it difficult to be loving.

When you practice doing all four steps, your children must rethink their behavior. They're used to thinking, "As long as I keep an adult busy with me, then I'm loved." Now they see that they're loved without the adult having to "keep busy" with them.

> As a father talked across the fence in his backyard to his neighbor, his daughter Teresa kept interrupting him. His goal was for her to wait patiently until he finished. He wanted her to say politely, "Excuse me," as he had previously taught her to do. However, Teresa had other plans. She began whining immediately, "Daaaddy!" Dad kept on talking with his neighbor, and he did not talk to Teresa or make eye contact with her. He lovingly started rubbing her back as she stood whining beside him. She continued to whine for a few seconds and then stopped. She patiently waited for a break in their conversation and said very politely, "Excuse me, Daddy."

For successful redirection to occur, it's vital that you take time to be with your children when they are acting appropriately. There is less need for children to get negative attention when this need is getting met throughout the day.

Teach your child how to get your attention in appropriate ways. One mother taught her daughter to say, "I need some attention, Mommy," instead of acting out to get it. When her daughter said those words, Mom would either give her attention right then or she would negotiate a specific, agreed-on time to be with her child in a genuinely attentive way.

Busy parents can make "dates" with their children. Each child gets a separate date during the week. The dates may consist of breakfast, lunch with the child at school, roller-skating, fishing, and so on. These one-on-one times are essential. It's much easier for children to share intimate thoughts and feelings when they're alone with you in a relaxed atmosphere. If they feel they have a close relationship with you, they become more respectful and more cooperative.

Fathers often play "rough-and-tumble" with both their little sons and daughters. When their daughters start physically developing in the teen years, fathers frequently quit tumbling with them. It is important for fathers to replace this activity with some other activity so that their daughters don't feel abandoned. For example, one father started taking tennis lessons with his daughter. Another father started a nightly routine of reading a chapter in a novel they had picked out together.

Some questions to ask yourself if your child is attention seeking are:

- Am I not giving my child enough attention when his or her behavior is appropriate?
- Am I giving my child too much attention and not teaching him or her how to entertain herself?
- Am I not fully present when I do give him or her my attention?
- Am I giving him or her attention mostly when he or she misbehaves?

# 10

# Redirecting the Mistaken Goal of Power

Power does not corrupt. Fear corrupts.
Perhaps the fear of a loss of power.

—John Steinbeck

"Turn the TV off," Dad says to Jordan. "It's time for bed."

"Aw, Dad, let me finish watching this one show. It'll be over in thirty minutes," challenges Jordan.

"No, I said turn it off!" Dad demands with a stern look on his face.

"Why? I'll just watch fifteen minutes, OK? C'mon, let me watch it. You never let me stay up late anymore," Jordan protests.

Angrily, Dad points his finger at the TV. "Did you hear what I said, young man? I said off with the TV . . . NOW!"

Father feels angry and challenged. His natural inclination is to use more force. To help you tell the difference between the mistaken goals of power and attention, watch what your children do. When you reprimand children who are seeking attention, their misbehavior stops because they have achieved their goal. They have your attention. However, when you reprimand children who have the mistaken goal of power, their misbehavior usually escalates. Even if the behavior stops temporarily, they will adopt a defiant demeanor.

Being in a power struggle with your children is absolutely miserable and exhausting. You may be able to make them do what you want, but at what cost? Here are some reasons why it is essential for you to get out of and stay out of power struggles:

- Things can quickly escalate and get out control—that is, things get said and done that you regret.
- You lose sight of the bigger picture of what you want to be teaching your child.
- It hurts and creates resentment, hostility, and revenge.
- It builds a wall between the two of you.
- It creates dread of yet another power struggle on the horizon.
- It teaches your child an ineffective and unhealthy way to connect in relationships.
- You feel guilt ridden for using force to get your child to cooperate.
- Winners and losers are created, and no one likes to lose.
- You frequently walk on eggshells to avoid yet another conflict.
- Power struggles often intensify as the child gets older.

All these factors basically suck the joy out of your relationship.

When the child's goal is power, typically parents feel angry, challenged, and that their authority is being threatened, or that they want to force their child to do something—it is power struggle *on*! Being attentive to your feelings is half the battle. Once you are aware of your feelings, you can prevent power struggles from happening.

*The most common way people give up their power is by thinking they don't have any.*
—Alice Walker

Feeling powerless and defeated are additional features of power struggles. The tools in this chapter will help you take back your power in a healthy way, so you don't have to overpower or acquiesce.

Children need to feel powerful, valuable, and influential. When we do the following things, we create a feeling of lost power:

- Punish
- Threaten
- Slap, spank, pinch
- Criticize
- Name-call
- Compare them to others
- Withdraw love
- Shame

Remember what I said about self-acceptance. This is where you take a deep breath and say, "Boy, I am glad I am here looking for something new!" instead of beating yourself up for having used any of these tactics in the past.

There are two distinctive sections to this chapter: preemptive work, and what to do when you are smack in the middle of a conflict.

## Preemptive Work

When in a power struggle, put a governor on your temper, step away from your child, take some deep breaths, and try one of the following techniques to redirect a power struggle.

### *Learn to Pause* **Before** *You Parent*

Instead of merely reacting to our children's antics, we get better results when we pause and calm down before we respond. Here are some reasons why this is so important:

- **Knee-jerk reactions are averted.** These reactions usually draw from the well of our unconscious where all old parenting styles lie, such as lashing out, yelling, nagging, threatening, and so on.
- **Pausing helps us to manage our anger better.** Who doesn't want to tame his or her angry outbursts? Every time we are

calm instead of angry, we strengthen the wiring in our brain for more patience.

- **Pausing allows us to be more conscious.** We can then be more present and creative.
- **Your child is watching.** Children look to us to learn how to solve problems.

Pausing creates a powerful window of time between the stimulus—our child's acting out—and our response. It is powerful in that we get to choose how we want to react. We have no choice when we are simply reacting. We also get to determine how long our pause will last. It can be a few seconds or a few days.

During the pause, do something to soothe yourself. Take some deep breaths, count backward from ten, say a mantra, pray, leave the room, or scream into a pillow. From that peace you will find an answer, a solution. This a good time to ask yourself, "What result do I want to create here?"

## Check and Redirect Your Intentions

Before you enter an altercation with your child, a helpful tip is to ask yourself, "What is my intention here?" Your unconscious intentions may be about:

- Wanting to control your child.
- Concern with whether your child makes you look good.
- Needing to avoid conflict.
- A desire for your child to like you.
- Needing to teach your child a lesson.
- Wanting to hurt back.

I have done all of these! When we are unaware of our intentions, it is easy to get duped into struggles over power. We are most effective when our intentions are about connecting and being in the moment. When we are in the moment, we will know when to teach life skills, be supportive, understand our children's needs, listen intently, follow through on a limit we have set, or simply sit there quietly. Before you approach your child, it helps to check your intentions as often as possible. Doing this can preempt a struggle.

> *Ultimately, the only power to which man should aspire is that which he exercises over himself.*
> —ELIE WIESEL

## Rules Without Relationship = Rebellion

We all have a deep need for connection. Having a meaningful relationship with your child is paramount to your child's willingness to cooperate and thus help you prevent power struggles. Parents who have too many rules and are too busy to play, have fun, and find ways to connect will be met with more resistance than parents who spend quality time with their children. This doesn't mean you have to spend hours with your children. However, it is crucial to be present and not think about anything else when you are with them.

## Know Your Child

Watch how your children react in different situations. When your children get hungry or tired, do they become irritable and less cooperative? Which children do they play best with? Do they play better at someone else's house? Or do they play better in neutral territory such as a park where they do not feel they have to protect their territory? How long can they play with another child before they start needing their own space? When your teenagers come home from school, is it best to allow them some time before you discuss their day? Or do they respond better right before bedtime?

Watch your children's patterns to know when they are really "misbehaving" or just physically uncomfortable. It is much more helpful if you can get your children's basic needs met as quickly as possible rather than getting into power struggles

## *Know Your Child's Triggers*

I frequently give parents the assignment to keep a journal of what things set their children off. If you know their triggers, you can help prevent your children from losing it.

Here are a few things that might trigger your children. Check the triggers your children have from the list below:

- ☐ Overstimulation
- ☐ Overtired
- ☐ Transitions
- ☐ Certain clothing like labels on shirts
- ☐ Playdates at home
- ☐ Smells
- ☐ Loud noises
- ☐ Being rushed
- ☐ Fluorescent lights
- ☐ Certain foods
- ☐ Too much screen time
- ☐ Certain textures
- ☐ A time of the day
- ☐ Other_____

Here are some questions to ask yourself:
- How do they react when triggered?
- How do you react when they are triggered?
- What is one small thing you could you do to prevent this from happening?

## *Give Notice of Time*

You've been invited to a special party for a visiting dignitary. There are many interesting people to talk to, and you're circulating from one stimulating group of people to another. You settle into a conversation with a woman from Russia who is telling you about Russian social customs. Suddenly, your husband grabs your hand, forces your coat on you, and says, "Come on. It's time to go home."

How would you feel? Maybe disrespected and violated? Children have similar feelings when we demand that they make an abrupt shift in what they're doing so we can get them to do things such as leave a friend's house or go to bed. You will have fewer power struggles if you give them a friendly notice, such as, "We will be leaving in five minutes" or "Bedtime is in ten minutes. I'll set the timer." Notice how much better you would have felt toward your husband if he had said in the above example, "I would like to leave in fifteen minutes."

## *Plan in Advance*

You can avoid last-minute hassles by planning ahead. For example, have your child get school clothes, books, lunch, and so on ready the night before. While everyone is calm, instead of the time of conflict, you can discuss what clothes will be worn, whether homework is finished, see if there is enough lunch meat for sandwiches, or find out if you're expected to supply cupcakes. Children are more cooperative and pleasant when they can go at their own pace and they know what to expect.

Here is how one mom use advanced planning to minimize or circumvent meltdowns from happening.

> Hailey had difficulty with her daughter Maddy when it was time for her to transition from preschool to home. Maddy would often run off and hide when she saw Mom at pickup time. Realizing Maddy was having a problem with the transition, Mom devised a routine to help her. Together they created this plan: Maddy could say goodbye to her class's pet gerbil, go down the slide once (not two or three times). And then she could take her shoes and socks off immediately when she got into the car. This routine significantly minimized the struggle to get Maddy home.

## Know Your Triggers

Fighting among the kids would drive me crazy. It was one of my triggers, and as a result, I was often reactive when they fought. My brother was ten years older than me and picked on me incessantly. As a result, I was especially sensitive when my older son picked on my daughter. Discovering this trigger helped me to unplug and see how my reaction was perpetuating the problem.

> Teens tend to develop an annoying stage where they think they are always right and become know-it-alls. Isaac was having vehement arguments with his son, Weston. Dad would get riled up even though he knew this was a normal stage of development and it would eventually pass.
>
> When we explored this trigger, Isaac discovered that his father always had to be right and refused to admit when he was wrong. As a result, Isaac had emotionally pulled away from his own father. Dad didn't want his son to disturb their relationship over needing to be right. Dad realized that he was too invested in his son's learning that being right wasn't more important than the relationship.
>
> This awareness led Isaac to quit arguing with his son. Now he simply says, "You might be right about that," and drops the subject.

What are your triggers? Perhaps it's disrespect, sass, lying, or homework issues. Knowing your triggers can help you to prepare for them and find a different way to respond rather than be reactionary.

It is also helpful to know your partner's triggers so you can help each other. Having someone on your team who can gently assist you by bringing your awareness to these situations can be very powerful.

## Find Useful Ways for Your Child to Feel Powerful and Valuable

As I mentioned earlier, if children aren't given appropriate ways to feel powerful, they will get this need met by finding inappropriate ways. Find appropriate methods for your children to feel valuable, powerful, and influential. Put a check by one thing you will do today and a smiley face by something you are already doing.

- ☐ Ask for their advice.
- ☐ Put them in positions of leadership like leading a family meeting, planning session, or family meal.
- ☐ Ask their opinion.
- ☐ Give them choices.
- ☐ Put them in charge of an important task.
- ☐ Have them teach you something you don't already know.
- ☐ Give a designated amount of money to pay for an item the family needs.
- ☐ Have them help with the family budget.
- ☐ Ask, "How can I give them more appropriate power right now?"

During a power struggle, our mind's overriding thought is, "How can I make them stop?" Try a new approach. Change the question to, "How can I give them more appropriate power right now?" Children who feel powerful have no need to struggle for power.

When Tyler was three years old, he and I went grocery shopping around 5:30 PM. Big mistake! I was tired, and he was tired. I was in a hurry to get home to prepare supper, so I put him in the shopping cart to expedite the shopping trip. As I hurried down each aisle grabbing what I needed, Tyler began throwing the groceries out of the cart. At first I said calmly, "Tyler, please stop." He ignored me and continued throwing things out of the cart. Then I said more harshly, "Tyler, *stop it!*" As my voice rose in anger, his behavior escalated. Next, he took my purse and dumped the entire contents all over the floor. I grabbed his small arms. I wanted to shake him!

At that instant, I understood how child abuse occurs. I took a few steps back and counted to ten, which is a method I use to calm myself. As I was counting, I realized that Tyler had no power in this situation. He had been forced into a cold, hard shopping-cart seat as his harried mother rushed through the store picking up items he didn't even care about. I asked myself, "What can I do to make Tyler feel more powerful in this situation?"

I decided one thing I could do instantly was to ask Tyler's advice about shopping. "Do you think Snoopy [our dog] would like this kind of dog food or that kind? What vegetables do you think Dad would like?" By the time we moved into the next aisle, I was amazed at how cooperative Tyler had become. I thought someone had swapped children with me, but I knew it was I who had changed, not my son.

Sometimes when the situation is stressful, such as when the struggle is a matter of safety, it feels like exerting our power is going to be more effective than addressing the need. It is hard to remember this when we are stressed. At these times we are more likely to be tempted to fall back to exerting our power.

Here is another example:

Three-year-old Katy would not put on her seat belt and keep it fastened. Her mother would get to work late, feeling tired and frustrated even though the day had hardly begun. No matter how much she argued and threatened, Katy would not cooperate. So Mom changed her approach. She decided to make Katy the "Captain of the Seat Belts." Mom could not start the car until Katy told her that all the other people in the car had their seat belts on. Katy felt important and powerful because she was now in charge of whether they could depart. Her behavior changed from defiant to cooperative overnight.

These methods will also help to rectify relationships that are already tense and need repair. Here is an example of one stepmother's tense relationship:

A stepmother was struggling with establishing a relationship with her fourteen-year-old stepdaughter, Anna. They were often engaging in battles of wills. Stepmom decided to ask Anna to assist her in choosing some new clothes for her husband. Stepmom vulnerably shared with Anna her lack of knowledge about current fashions and asked for her advice. Anna reluctantly agreed to help. The shopping trip provided fashionable clothes for Dad, but more important, it helped Anna feel valuable. It was the turning point in the relationship between stepmother and stepdaughter.

Parents think of incredibly creative ways to give their children power when they put their minds to it. One of my favorites is this father's story:

> A father I was coaching had a seventeen-year-old son whose grades were slipping from As and Bs to Cs and Ds. Also, the two were having altercations over just about everything. I asked Dad how his son was valuable to him. His response was, "Valuable? He's a pain in the @##!" I coached him on how important it is for a child to feel valuable in the family. And then I asked the question again, only in a different way. I asked, "What is something your son is really good at that you might be able to use his help on?" He thought for a while and said, "Well, my son used to be really good at math, and I sure could use some help with the accounting in my flower shop." Dad proceeded to ask for his son's help, and within a month, his son's grades started going back up. Within three months, their relationship drastically changed because the two of them now had the flower shop in which they could bond.

## Teach Your Child How to Say No Respectfully

Are you kidding? Why would I do that? Some power struggles occur because children have not been taught how to say no respectfully. Most of us were raised to do as our parents told us, whether we liked it or not. However, children who aren't allowed to say no directly say it indirectly. They can say it by dawdling, forgetting, or doing a job ineffectively so that you either must finish it for them or you don't bother to ask them again. Some children even get sick. It is more difficult to deal with a no that is said under the table than one said directly. If children can say no directly, their communication is honest and clear.

How many times have you gotten yourself in trouble because you felt you couldn't say no? Allowing your children to say it won't cost you anything because they are already saying it indirectly. Think of the benefits for children who can say no. They can say it to peers who want them to participate in drugs, sex, stealing, vandalism, hurtful activities, and other situations where someone wishes to coerce them.

If you don't teach your children, who will? The pressure to be liked by parents early in a child's life is probably equivalent to the peer pressure they will feel as a teen, so what a great time to learn and practice saying no!

On occasion I asked my son to help clean up the house. Sometimes he said, "No, I don't want to," and that wasn't OK with me. At those times, I said, "But it's important to me to get the house picked up because we're having friends over tonight." So we negotiated a win-win solution. Tyler said, "I'll watch Brianna [his little sister] for you instead." Then I had the free time to clean up. We both won.

As odd as this may sound, when you allow your children to say no, they are more willing to cooperate. You have given them power in the situation, and that makes them feel like they don't need to defy you.

## Make Sure Your Expectations Are Reasonable

"Arden refuses to clean his room," complained a mom I was coaching. He was four years old. I explained to the mother that asking her four-year-old to clean his room was overwhelming for him. Children can act resistant when they are frustrated or overwhelmed.

You will set yourself and your child up for success by breaking tasks down into accomplishable bites. In this case, Mom could ask her son to put all his blocks away. After that, put away all his Legos. A four-year-old needs guidance to learn *how* to clean a room; make sure your requests are age appropriate.

A good rule of thumb is to wait until you see your children demonstrate doing a task consistently before you can expect that they can do it and before you add a new task.

## *Use Appropriate Timing*

How do you feel when someone interrupts you while you are in the middle of something you consider to be important? I would get annoyed. Our kids don't like being interrupted when they are doing something that is important to them either. Ask yourself, "Is this a good time to ask him or her to do this? Or am I going to be met with resistance? When would be a better time?" For example, when my daughter was little, she was usually a grump in the morning. I learned to wait until she had breakfast and had time to acclimate to being awake before I would make a request.

A helpful question to ask yourself is, "Where in my children's schedule am I not respecting their sense of timing?"

## *Avoid the Witching Hour*

What is your witching hour? Most families have one. For some, it is the trip on the way home from school; for others, it is the hour before dinner. And for some, it is bedtime. I noticed with my children that if they weren't in bed by 8:30 PM, bedtime became a nightmare. Determine what your witching hour is. Create a plan so that you can get a grip on the chaos.

One mom noticed her hangry (hungry + tired = hangry) daughter would lose it when Mom would pick her up from school nearly every day. Mom would ask sweetly, "What did you do in school today?"

"Nothin'," the daughter would mutter.

"How could you do nothing all day?" the annoyed mother would ask. And off they would go into a nasty scenario.

To circumvent this problem, Mom decided she would bring her daughter a healthy snack and plant it on her car seat. She would not start a conversation until her daughter had eaten her snack. Problem solved!

Here is an example of dealing with the witching hour of getting kids off to school in the morning.

Mom heard herself yelling, "Hurry up! We're going to be late" ad nauseam, only to find her kids *still* dawdling! She decided that she would start playing "Beat the Clock." She made her family aware of the game. She timed how long it took them to get out the door. Each morning Mom would report yesterday's time, and then she would challenge them by playfully asking, "How much time do you think we can shave off this morning?" They not only got out the door faster but she also noticed that they began to make it a team effort, one where kids were helping other kids get their stuff together.

Whenever possible, make things a team effort. This gives children a sense of belonging. Getting that need met aids in diminishing acting out to get power.

When is your witching hour? Put a check by the one that is most irritating to you now.

- ☐ Getting the kids up
- ☐ Getting the kids dressed
- ☐ Getting them out the door in the morning
- ☐ Picking them up from school
- ☐ Right before dinner
- ☐ Bedtime

What is one small intervention you can take to make this time more pleasant? Think about how you could make these segments of time less stressful and more fun.

## Make Agreements Ahead of Time

Do you go crazy when you get into the store and your children want to buy candy and toys? Or when you have to run an errand with your children and the minute you get where you need to be they start whining to leave? An effective way to deal with this kind of problem is to make an agreement with your children ahead of time. One determining factor for success in making agreements is that you keep your word. If you don't keep your word, your children will learn to distrust you and refuse to cooperate.

A mom owned her own business and would frequently take her child with her to work. Mother made an agreement ahead of time with her child: "We will be here for only fifteen minutes, and then we'll go." Her daughter would sit and draw while Mom worked.

Eventually, Mom began to stretch the fifteen minutes because her child was playing so happily. The little girl figured out that they were staying longer and longer. She started putting up a fuss when Mom wanted to take her to the office. When Mom realized what was happening, she began to honor her commitment to leave at the agreed-on time. Her daughter gradually began to trust her again.

If you plan on going shopping, tell your children ahead of time how much money you're willing to spend on them. Tell them that you're unwilling to spend any more than that amount. It works best to give them the money. Design a consequence for what happens if they bug you to buy more than the designated amount. One possibility is that the next time you go shopping, they will have to stay home, but they can try again the following trip.

Here is another example regarding making agreements:

Ashley found herself at an impasse with her son, Max, about the amount of time he could play on his favorite educational game. So they negotiated an agreement. He could play his game twice a day for thirty minutes. Mom was willing to allow this if he didn't put up a fight when she told him his time was up.

If your child develops a habit of breaking his agreement, prevent this from happening by using the phrase, "What should happen if you don't keep your agreement?" In this case, Max said, "You can take the game and put it away until tomorrow."

Max did end up breaking his agreement. Mom was prepared for the test. She took his game and said in a friendly voice, "You can try again tomorrow." When I followed up with them two weeks later, Max had consistently been giving the game to Mom without a fuss. She happily reported, "It's like magic. I haven't had a problem with him since!"

It helps to give a concise lesson on how important it is to keep agreements and how keeping agreements builds trust. Talk about what the consequences are for people who continually break their agreements. But keep it short! Children learn to tune us out when we talk too much.

## Make Sure You Have an Agreement

"Yeah, sure," was Austin's response to Mom's request to take out the trash. Unfortunately, Mom ignored her son's tone of voice and his dismissive demeanor. She proceeded to think she had her son's agreement, but she actually didn't. Be aware of children who just say whatever they think you want to hear to get you off their back. If you don't, you will set yourself and your child up for failure.

Mom would have been more successful if she had said, "It doesn't seem like you are into taking out the trash right now. What's getting in your way?"

"I just started this game," answers Austin.

"I get that. When would you be willing to do it?" asks Mom.

"Can I do it right after dinner?" asks Austin.

"That works. Next time I ask you to do something you don't want to do, just be honest with me, not sassy. We can work things out respectfully."

## Get Their Attention Before You Make a Request

"Madelyn," Mom calls out from the kitchen, "it's time for dinner." Madelyn ignores the request. Mom amps up her tone of voice. "Madelyn, it's time for dinner." No response from Madelyn. Angrily, Mom grabs a crying Madelyn by the arm and forces her to the dinner table, mumbling, "I don't know when you are ever going to listen!"

What went wrong? Mom did not have her daughter's attention before she made the request. You will win more cooperation if you get close to children, get on their eye level (don't tower over them), and call their name once—not two or three times. Then pause and wait until they make eye contact with you before you make your request. It can also help to ask them what they heard you say.

## What to Do in the Middle of a Power Struggle

All the advice so far is preparation to keep power struggles at bay in general. But when the unavoidable happens, here are steps to take in the moment.

### *Let Go of Your Fixed Position*

I am sure you have heard the adage "Pick your battles." Parents frequently get locked into the idea that things should go a certain way. If they are not done that way, and when we want it done, we get freaked out.

> Three-year-old Mia was busy squishing the blueberries on the floor, captivated by their popping sound. At first Mom wanted to put a halt to this activity. But then she realized her daughter was experimenting, so she let go of her position and decided to join her daughter's frivolity. They had a delightful time giggling and feeling the sensations between their toes. When they were done, they cleaned up their mess together. Mom also explained that from now on blueberries were for eating not squishing.

If you were raised in a family that wasn't allowed to make messes, situations like the one above may seem challenging. However, the outcome can quite bonding. Ask yourself, "Will this matter five years from now?" or "Is this a critical battle for me to fight?" If the answer is no, let it go.

To let go does not mean you don't care. It means you are letting go of your investment in or grip over the situation and trusting that everything will work out.

Where is there an area with your child in which it would be better for both of you if you let go?

## Ask, "What Would You Be Willing to Do?"

It was chore time at our house. Tyler's job was to take the dishes out of the dishwasher that day. He said that he didn't want to do that chore. So I asked, "What would you be willing to do?" He said that he would be willing to vacuum instead. I headed off a power struggle!

Sometimes it is important to have your children do things they don't want to do. It helps build their character. However, that morning I chose to pick my battles and emptying the dishwasher wasn't one of them.

## Use Distraction

When you are in the middle of a power struggle, use distraction. For example, if your toddler is in a car seat throwing a tantrum, ask, "Did I tell you what I saw on the way to work today?" or "Look at that giant dump truck!" One father learned to take his crying toddler outside to one particular tree. For some odd reason, his son would then settle down. Do this early in the tantrum. If you wait too long, distraction is less likely to be effective.

## Give Children Space

Some children, and even some adults, do better when you give them time to process the information you are giving them. For example, if you have asked your son to clean his room, don't hover over him until he starts heading to his room. Give him several minutes before you follow up.

## Don't Waffle

Let your yeses be yes and your nos be no. When we are unclear about a situation, our children can sense this and may take their opportunity to push their limits. Waffling sends them a mixed and confusing message. Learn to get clear about what you want to have happen.

- Where are you giving your child a mixed message?
- What would it take for you to not waffle?

## *Give Yourself Time to Respond*

Sometimes we feel pressured to answer the demands of our children right away. When we respond too quickly, our decisions are often not the best ones.

> I was coaching a father of a teenage girl. He complained about how they argued almost every morning before school. The daughter would inevitably ask him for permission to do something at the very last minute, such as riding to school with a friend. The problem was that the father sometimes didn't know the details, like who this friend was. More important, he enjoyed connecting with her on the ride to school. Their arguments ended in shouting matches and door slamming.
>
> Dad felt pressured to answer his daughter's requests right away, which resulted in some poor decision-making and a hostile teen. I suggested to him that he tell his daughter that he needed five minutes to think over all his decisions. This helped, much to his relief. His mornings became calmer, and he felt more confident in his decision-making.

Teens tend to be impulsive and pressure parents for immediate answers. You don't have to fall prey to their instant gratification, nor do you have to do battle over it.

## *Use Win-Win Negotiation*

It is easy for children to feel like we are against them and have all the power. Win-win negotiation helps your children feel like you are on their side and teaches them valuable life skills.

Most of us were not taught the concept of win-win negotiation as children. Our experience involves win-lose or lose-lose situations. The most effective negotiations are those where both parties strive for a solution in which both win and are happy with the result. To arrive at such a solution, each person must listen intently to what the other person wants while staying committed to his or her own wish or need.

The essence of negotiation is that each party thinks of ideas that will allow both parties to get what they want. Neither tries to talk the other out of or into anything different from what each wants. Both parties keep thinking of solutions until each has exactly what he or she wants. Synergy is experienced and delightful surprises are arrived at because two heads are better than one.

> I was going to do a lecture in my hometown, and I asked my son, who was eight at the time, to support me by going along. As I was headed out the door for the lecture, I glanced down at Tyler's jeans. There, poking out of a large hole, was his knee. My heart sank. I promptly asked him to change. He said no, and I found myself engaged in a power struggle with him.
>
> As soon as I realized what we were doing, I stopped. After a moment's thought, I decided to use win-win negotiation skills. I asked Tyler why he was unwilling to change his pants. He said that friends of his were going to be at the lecture. All the kids who wanted to be cool wore holes in their jeans, and he wanted to be cool too. I explained my position: "It's important for me that you win. I want you to win. However, I will be embarrassed in front of all these people if you have holes in your jeans. How can I win too?"
>
> I couldn't think of a solution, but Tyler thought for a moment and said, "How about this? How about if I wear a good pair of pants over my jeans? Then, when I'm around your friends, I won't have holes. When I'm around my friends, I'll take them off." I marveled at Tyler's creativity. I said, "What a great solution! I would have never thought of that. Thanks for negotiating with me."

Here is an example with my toddler:

> Three-year-old Brianna and I were taking a bath. Brianna was happy with just a little water, but I wanted more water. I could tell we would

be headed for a power struggle. I asked, "I hear you want little water, and I want big water. How can we both win?"

She thought for a few seconds and said, "How about if we have big water while you're in the tub with me? And then when you get out, I'll have little water."

"Brilliant," I exclaimed.

Children can be far more creative than us adults sometimes!

Negotiations should start by asking children what they want. Listen with the intent to find a way that you will help them win. Then state what you want, being clear and concise. The phrase that is helpful to use during negotiation is, "It's important for me that you win. I want you to win. How can I win too?"

You may have to ask, "How can we *both* win?" several times. Keep negotiating until you are both happy with the solution.

The outcome you are striving for is that both people are happy with the solution. If one person is not pleased, he or she is likely to sabotage the agreement.

Warning: Win-win negotiation can be time consuming. It is more time efficient to just tell the child how things will be—but this is not relationship efficient. If the two of you cannot agree, table the conversation, and set a time to renegotiate. This gives everyone more time to reflect on the solution.

Once your family gets the hang of win-win negotiation, the process gets easier. At some point, all that you will have to say is "win-win" and your children will jump right on the task. When children get that you're interested in their winning, they're eager to help figure out ways that allow both of you to have what you want.

Win-win does not apply to all situations. There should be some things in your family that are nonnegotiable, and some negotiable things. Nonnegotiable items might be wearing seat belts, toddlers holding your hand as you cross the street, and bedtime, to name a few.

## Give Choices

Children need and want appropriate control over their lives. Giving your children a choice gives them a sense of control.

There are four types of choices:

1. Concrete choices. Would you like to start with your math or science?
2. Choices with incentive. If you choose to come now, we will have time to read three books.
3. Playful choices. Would you like a piggyback ride to bed, or do you want to be a wheelbarrow?
4. Choices with a consequence. You may put your seat belt on by yourself, or I will help you.

Here is an example of where a dad could have used a choice with a consequence:

> Dad and his two-year-old son were in a doughnut shop. The boy was wandering around in front of the doorway. Dad was concerned that his son might hurt himself or become a nuisance to the entering customers. He said, "Michael, come here!" Michael seemed to enjoy his act of defiance and continued to absorb himself in the commotion around the door. Again, Dad demanded, "Michael, come here right now or we're leaving!" Dad finally picked up his son and brought him over to the table. Michael went back to the door when he could wiggle away from Dad's clutches. Dad yelled, "Now, Michael, I'm not going to tell you again, get away from that door. . . . If I've told you once, I've told you a thousand times. MICHAEL!"

Dad never did follow through with his promise to leave. Dad's words would have been more effective if he had given the situation his full attention. He could have given Michael a choice—"Would you like to stay beside me or leave the doughnut shop?"—after his first request was ignored. If the child hadn't come away from the door,

Dad could have immediately followed through by picking his child up and leaving the shop. Then Michael would have learned that Dad means what he says. If Dad doesn't want to leave, then he shouldn't give Michael that choice.

**Note**: When you offer this choice, use a friendly tone of voice. Otherwise, it can be perceived as a threat by the child.

Giving choices teaches children the valuable life lesson that when challenging situations occur, they can explore their options. They do not have to be victims of circumstances. Children who are given choices learn to make decisions on their own, are less dependent on their parents and other adults, and are less rebellious. They also learn to recognize the connection between their decisions and the consequences they experience.

When you offer a choice, keep these cautions in mind:

- Be sure that both the choices you give are acceptable to you.
- If children won't choose either option, offer another choice that allows you to take action. For example, "Would you like to walk or would you like me to carry you?"
- If your children still do not choose, assume they don't want the freedom to choose. Choose for them and act. In the example above, pick them up gently and carry them from the room.

Some other examples of simple choices are these:

- "Would you like to dress in the house or in the car?"
- "Would you prefer to brush your teeth now or after we read?"

Be sure that neither of the choices you offer is a punishment, for then there is no choice. For example, "Would you like to be quiet or go to your room?" offers no real choice.

Sometimes it's hard to think of choices to offer children. This may be because you don't feel like you have many choices in your own life. Practice giving yourself more options.

Doctors who have learned about redirecting children's behavior have eased the tensions of office visits considerably by giving choices. When children need a shot, they are given a choice of which arm to get it in or they can have a choice of colorful Band-Aids. They can decide whether to sit by themselves or sit in the parent's lap as the shot is given. Even though they may not be happy about the shot, the choices give them some control and responsibility in a situation where they might have felt out of control.

## Make It Fun!

Children love to have fun. The more you make things fun, the more cooperation you will win. Instead of barking, "Quit fighting," make the situation fun by turning up some loud music and dancing with them. When we allow ourselves to get stressed out and overwhelmed, we are not fun to be with.

Make life lessons fun for you and your child. For example, try singing "No" instead of speaking in your usual admonishing voice or try developing a funny character (perhaps Donald Duck) who makes requests to do things, such as household chores.

Here is how I made homework fun for my son:

> I was struggling with Tyler over his homework. He was supposed to be learning the multiplication tables, and we were getting nowhere fast. Finally, I asked Tyler, "When you're learning something, do you need to see it, hear it, or feel it?" He said that he needed all three ways. So I took out an oblong cake pan and put a layer of his father's shaving cream in the bottom. I wrote the problem in the shaving cream and Tyler wrote the answer. I was amazed! He went from being a child who couldn't care less about what 9 x 7 equaled to a child who was rapidly writing the answers with as much glee as if he had been let loose in a toy store. And, of course, the homework session ended in an uproarious shaving cream fight between us!

You may think you don't have time to come up with unique ways for your child to learn, or that you aren't creative. I urge you to throw these self-limiting thoughts out the window. The shaving cream technique not only was an easy way to help Tyler learn but it also became valuable bonding time for us. It certainly was better than the pulling-teeth method of multiplication drills.

## Act, Don't Yak

Did I mention that most parents talk too much? I think you are getting my point. This is one of the hardest concepts for parents to change.

> Mom was at the beach with her daughters, who were seven and ten years old. The last time they were at the beach, when Mom said it was time to go, the girls argued for about fifteen minutes. They were all in bad moods by the time they left.
>
> The next time it was time to leave the beach, Mom told the girls that they would be leaving in ten minutes. She also gave them a two-minute departure warning. After the two minutes passed, Mom said once, "It's time to go," and started heading to the car. The girls ran to catch up.

Notice that Mom did not threaten to leave. She didn't say, "If you don't come right now, I'm leaving you." It is never a good idea to threaten to leave your child.

It is helpful to ask yourself, "What action can I take instead of talking?" Our children listen to our actions more than they listen to our words.

Here is another example:

> Dad was furious when he found sixteen-year-old Angela and her boyfriend in her bedroom with the door shut again. Dad had told her numerous times to leave her bedroom door open when she had her boyfriend over. He decided he needed to take some action.
>
> After he calmed down (you never want to act out of anger), he got out his screwdriver and proceeded to take the door off the hinges. Angela was furious. He said she could have the door back the following week. Later, when she calmed down, he told her he had taken off the hinges for two reasons. One was, "As a father, it is my job to protect you even though you don't feel like you need protection. I

know you must feel like I am just trying to control you, and I hope someday you will see this as an act of love. The second reason is I felt disrespected, and that is not OK."

Several months later, after Angela had broken up with her boyfriend, she thanked Dad because her boyfriend had been pushy, and she was having trouble saying no to him.

You can't force your child to do anything. (Technically, you could overpower your child, but this will only disturb the relationship.) Concentrate on what action you can take.

- What is one situation in which you are talking too much?
- What action could you take instead?

## Use Signals

Again, to cut down on your yakking, devise a signal between the two of you that lets the other person know that he or she is doing "that thing" again. Children (and adults) are seldom aware of their own annoying behaviors. Using a signal can be a nonjudgmental way of helping to correct the behavior. It is best if the child chooses the signal, and that it would not be embarrassing if someone on the outside saw it. Here is an example:

Brianna was eleven and was usually a very grateful child. She also moved from one activity to another very quickly. As a result, she would often forget to say thank you to her host when visiting. At a time when we were not in conflict, I said to Brianna, "You are such a grateful child, and I think you are unaware that you sometimes forget to say thank you when you leave your friend's house. Would you like me to give you a reminder?" She answered yes. Our signal was for me to touch her on the elbow if she forgot.

Several weeks later, we were leaving her friend's house. We walked down the sidewalk, and she hadn't said thank you. We got all the way to the car, and she was about to get in the car when I touched her elbow. She looked at me with a flashback of our agreement and called out, "Thank you, Ms. Anderson. I had so much fun." Power struggle averted!

Signals are helpful between parents too. We used the touch on the elbow as a signal to go into the bedroom to handle disagreements about managing our kids.

• What situation could you use a signal for?

## *Do Role Reversal*

Children typically are unaware of how they sound and how they affect others. It can be enlightening to them to reverse roles during a power struggle. Please do not do this in a mean-spirited way. It must be done playfully.

> Armani kept poking his mother when he wanted her attention. Mom had told him that she didn't like being poked and she had told him how to get her attention without poking her. But he kept poking her. She decided to reverse roles with him and started poking him in a playful but annoying way. When Armani told Mom that he didn't like this, Mom started laughing and said, "Now you know how I feel!"
>
> A few days later, Armani started poking Mom again. She smiled and gently moved his hand. He gave Mom a knowing look and stopped poking her.

## *Do the Unexpected*

Children generally have their parents figured out at a very early age. They know what to expect. When you do the unexpected, your child no longer gets your usual response to the behavior at hand. As a result, you break the pattern of the power struggle.

> Addison had two children, ten and fourteen, who would always fight when they did the dishes. Mom would then get engaged and try to get them to stop, to no avail.
>
> While taking the parenting course, she got the idea to do the unexpected. That night when the kids started fighting, Mom grabbed the paper towels and wet them down. Then she began flinging them at the fighting kids, laughing as she tossed them. They were shocked

and stopped fighting and started launching the wet paper towels back at Mom and each other. The had an uproarious time and forgot about the fight.

One mom was having a power struggle with her small son over taking his bath. As usual, no end to the struggle was in sight. She noticed two squirt guns in her son's bedroom. Grabbing the squirt guns, she yelled invitingly, "Let's have a squirt-gun fight in the bathtub!" Both had a great time laughing in the tub, and Mom accomplished her goal.

Maybe your children are too old for this bath method, but the purpose of the example is to stretch your imagination. Make parenting more fun for yourself and your child in as many ways as you can think of. While you're defusing power struggles in the present, you're also creating memories of family fun for the future. Ask yourself:

- What do I normally do in this situation?
- Would this be an appropriate time to do the unexpected?

## Give in Fantasy What You Can't Give in Reality

You can't always give your children what they want, nor should you. However, one tool to put in your toolbox is to provide them in fantasy what you don't want them to have in reality. This concept can help you avoid a lot of altercations. Here's an example:

Audrey was three, and she really wanted an ice cream cone. It was right before dinner, and Mom wisely knew that ice cream would ruin her appetite. Mom said, "You can't have ice cream because we will soon be having dinner. But, if you could have ice cream, what kind would you get?"

"I'd get cookies and cream," her daughter exclaimed.

Mom replied, "Oh, that sounds really yummy. Would you put it in a waffle cone?"

This conversation seemed to satisfy Audrey. She felt like her mom really heard her request.

Mom didn't dismiss or diminish her child's desire. She simply engaged her daughter in fantasy.

## Give Empathy

Empathy includes helping children feel understood, heard, and accepted. When children feel misunderstood, unheard, and judged, they become more defiant. Try to really get your children. Put yourself in their shoes.

Instead of saying, "No, you can't buy that toy. It's too expensive," say, "I hear you *really* want that toy. You love toys that make those sounds. Let's put it on your birthday wish list right away when we get home."

## Focus on the Solution, Not on the Problem

*The secret of change is to focus all of your energy, not on fighting the old, but on building the new.*

—Socrates

Dwelling on the problem only promotes negative and stressful energy. It doesn't do any good. Where there is negative energy and stress, misbehavior generally rears its ugly head. When we dwell on the negative, we complain and blame others.

Stop judging and operating from a closed mindset that nothing is working. Instead, develop the open mindset: where there is a problem, there is always a solution.

Focus on finding the solution. If you are having difficulty, join a parenting class to get more ideas, bring the problem to a family meeting to brainstorm a solution, or read a parenting book. Don't get stuck in the mire; find a solution.

## Ask, "What Do You Need?"

Almost always, a power struggle is a child's attempt to get a need met—perhaps a need to feel heard, feel understood, or maybe feel some control over his or her life. We must address the need behind what appears to be misbehavior.

"What's wrong with you now?" are words often spoken by parents. How more nurturing would it be if we changed the question to, "What do you need?" At first, your children might not know what they need. You might have to give them a few suggestions, such as, do you need a hug, do you need some alone time, or do you need me to just listen? Gradually your children will be able to communicate to you what they need. When this happens, life becomes more manageable as they will tell you what they need instead of acting out to get their needs met.

This works with spouses too.

Brian, my hubby, was trying to get our teenage daughter's attention. She was lying on the couch with her earbuds in ignoring her father. During his next attempt, Brianna rolled her eyes in disgust.

I was watching the whole scenario from the kitchen. I could see his frustration mounting, and I knew this scene would not end well. So I asked Brian, "What do you need?"

His answer was surprising: "I need to feel connected to my daughter," he replied unhappily.

I asked sympathetically, "Is what you are doing working?"

"No," he responded sheepishly.

"How else could you get her attention?" I asked.

He thought for a moment and then sat at the end of the couch and started rubbing her feet, which was her favorite thing. Within seconds, Brianna took out her earbuds and started having a great conversation with her father.

## *Legitimize the Behavior*

Create an appropriate way for your children to do what they want and still hold the limits you have set. For example, "I am not willing to have you bike alone to your friend's house. But I would be willing to let you go if you can talk your older brother into going with you."

If you can legitimize their activity, you will eliminate the power struggle. Think creatively, as this parent did.

A mother of four children could not get them to quit writing graffiti on the walls, no matter what discipline strategies she used. So she wallpapered the children's bathroom with white wallpaper and told them that they could write whatever they wanted in their bathroom. When they were given permission, they confined their drawings to the bathroom, much to Mom's relief. Whenever I went to their house, I would use the kids' bathroom because it was the most interesting room in the house!

Below are two examples used in a classroom setting.

A teacher had a problem in her classroom with some disruptive kids who decided they were the pilots of paper airplanes. The classroom looked like a busy airport. She decided to make a bad situation into a learning opportunity and devoted some time to the study of aerodynamics. As part of the curriculum, the children had to make paper airplanes that demonstrated aerodynamic designs. Much to her amazement, the students' fascination with paper planes dwindled.

I was hired to consult with a Montessori school. The staff was having trouble because eight-year-old Alex was "terrorizing" the kids on the playground during recess. The teachers were at their wit's end trying to figure out what to do with him since they had tried everything. After interviewing Alex, I discovered that he loved chasing people. I gathered all the kids together and asked them, "Who here does not like to be chased?" Several kids raised their hands. Then I asked, "Who here does likes to be chased?" I asked all the kids who didn't like to be chased to raise their hand again. Then I reinforced the idea by saying, "Alex, these people do not like being chased. Are you willing to stop chasing them?" He agreed. Then I had all the people who wanted to be chased raise their hands again and said, "Alex, these people like it when you chase them, and you are allowed to chase all the people with their hands up." He needed a few reminders, but his "reign of terror" soon ended.

Here is an example of legitimizing with a teen:

> After an angry altercation, my teenage daughter yelled, "This family
> blows! I want to get my own apartment." Instead of reacting with a
> lecture on how ungrateful she was being, I said, "I get it. You're frus-
> trated and angry right now and you have had it with this family. And
> you wish you could have your own apartment! Do you want to check
> some out?" We googled local apartments and she noticed the prices.
> After looking over several apartments, she said reluctantly, "I had no
> idea how much apartments cost. I guess I'll stay here."

What made this situation work was that I was prepared for some
difficult challenges with my teenagers. I had researched quite a bit about
their developmental stages. I knew that around the age of sixteen they
would say and do things that would help them individuate from the
family. They do this push-pull thing where one minute they can't stand
you and the next minute they need you. You can feel like an emotional
yo-yo if you are not prepared.

Many teenagers go through a period feeling that adults are not on
their side. In the example above, I took her side and legitimized her
desire. I didn't resist her. The result was she was able to calm down,
and she apologized for her angry outburst. We ended up having a great
conversation about how difficult it was to be a teenager and wanting
to be more independent.

## Slow Down

A major cause of power struggles today is overscheduling. The more we
rush and are anxious to get things done, the more we put pressure on
our children to do things quickly. Children are not developmentally
ready to do everything quickly or in an organized manner. The more
we pressure them, the more resistant they become. This creates tension
in families, and tension is a fertile breeding ground for power struggles
and tantrums. Allow yourself enough time so that you don't have to
hurry your child.

## *Prayer or Quiet Time*

There were many times I had no clue what to do when my children and I got into power struggles. One of the most useful things I learned was to pray. Frequently my prayer was, "God help me! I feel like smacking this kid. I don't want to hit her, but I don't know what else to do. Help!" And then I would get quiet and listen. Sometimes an answer would come immediately. Sometimes it would come later in the form of a friend who had the same problem, advice from my hubby, or an article I read in a magazine. But it always came.

If you don't pray, become still and let your mind go blank. Don't try to fix the situation. Just go blank. When we are in the thick of things it is often difficult to find solutions because we are either frustrated or angry. We can't find viable solutions when we are entertaining negative emotions.

## *Withdraw from Conflict*

Get out of the conflict as quickly as you can to keep the situation from escalating. The more you let the momentum build, the harder it is to redirect. You don't want your power struggle to upgrade to category ten!

Since it takes two to fight, refuse to participate. If you stay in the conflict, you are likely to say or do something you will regret later. Harsh words said in anger can be very destructive to your relationship and are slow to fade from memory.

Have you ever played tug-of-war and had the other team let go of its side of the rope? The game wasn't fun anymore, was it? You had nothing to pull against. It is the same with a power struggle. When we do not give our children any energy to fight against, there is no reason to continue the battle. Here's an example:

> Thirteen-year-old Noah was getting into an argument with his mother every night about taking a bath. Sometimes these arguments lasted up to ninety minutes. Mom was exhausted. In our Redirecting Children's Behavior class, we suggested that she withdraw from the

conflict and not say anything about his bathing. To which she exclaimed, "He'll never take a bath if I do that!" We said, "Whose problem is that?" After more discussion, Mom promised to try the technique that week.

The next week she reported that her son didn't take a bath for three days, and he was really starting to reek. The third night he said to Mom, "You haven't said anything about taking a bath for three *whole days!*"

Mom answered lightly, "That's right, and I never will!"

He came back ten minutes later and asked, "Never ever?"

Mom responded, "Never ever!" Later that evening, Mom heard the bathwater running. He took a bath every night that week without Mom having to say anything.

What made this work was that Mom refused to engage, yet she remained cheerful and calm.

There may be times when you need to physically remove yourself from the conflict. It is a good time to remove yourself if you are having trouble disengaging or if your child is being petulant. Your bathroom is an excellent place to get a reprieve from your children's barrage of arguments because it is usually a private place. Perhaps you have a lock on your door. Play loud music or run water if you need to drown out the sound. Many parents have confessed that they have hidden in their pantry or car.

Use this method only after trying the earlier suggestions. It would be easy to use this method to overpower your child. But your intention here needs to be to break your habit of giving in.

You might be asking, "But what if your child follows you around to get you to engage?"

A mom and dad I was coaching had given in to their teenage boy one to many times. By now he had learned that if he harassed his parents long enough, they would give in. They had tried leaving the situation so that they wouldn't get into an argument or give in. But it was to no avail—the teen would follow them around. I suggested that they get in their car and drive around. When they came back, their son was more civil.

- In what current situation could you use this method of withdrawing from the conflict?

## Say, "I Love You Too Much to Argue with You!"

Do you have one of those children who is destined to be a lawyer? You know, the persistent one who is always bargaining for one more *everything*. Once you have decided not to extend your limit, you must stay firm; otherwise, such children will learn they can just wear you down to get what they want. You will be walked over, and your children may become entitled. One way to effectively disengage is to say, "I love you too much to argue with you! Let's talk again in ten minutes," and walk away (this works great with spouses too!). Make sure you come back in ten minutes like you promised.

## Use a Calm, Still Voice

I was giving Ingrid, my two-year-old German shepherd, a lesson from a professional dog trainer. He was teaching me how to get my dog to sit. I sweetly turned to her and told her to sit. Of course, you guessed it, she wagged her tail as if ignoring my request. So I said it louder: "Ingrid, sit." Same result. Then I significantly increased my decibels and sternly commanded, "INGRID, SIT!"

My trainer calmly sauntered over to me and said, "Kathryn, your dog is not deaf. Don't raise your voice. Calmly and firmly give the command and wait. If she doesn't do what you ask, repeat." I followed his directions, and after the third calm command, Ingrid sat.

Parents often use the same ineffective approach I did with Ingrid. We say things like, "Brush your teeth." "I said, brush your teeth!" "DID YOU HEAR WHAT I SAID, YOUNG LADY? I SAID, BRUSH YOUR TEETH. NOW!"

When we escalate our tone, we inadvertently teach children to think, "I don't have to pay attention to Mom until she yells!"

## Use One Word

To avoid needing to deliver your fifty-seventh lecture on why your child should feed his or her dog, use one word. So instead of saying, "You haven't fed your dog yet! How would you like it if I didn't feed you?" simply say your dog's name in a friendly tone of voice.

One word our family used was *redo*, which meant, "I want to hear what you are saying. What you are saying is very important to me. I just need to hear it in a more respectful tone." So instead of saying all of that, we would just say the word *redo*. Anyone could say it to whoever was being disrespectful. Yes, the kids said it to me on numerous occasions. This was quite helpful since I wasn't always aware when I was being snarky.

Another example:

One family noticed that they had a lot of angry altercations. At a family meeting, the issue was brought up. The family decided that anyone could say the word *break* whenever there was an angry outburst. When the persons involved heard that word, they were to take a break and come back later when they had calmed down to resolve the issue.

- What power struggle could you avoid by using one word?
- What would that one word be?

## Patiently Hold Out Your Hand When You Need to Get an Object Away

Have you ever had your young children grab your phone, Magic Marker, or any other object you don't want them to have? It's frustrating, isn't it? If you grab the object out of their hands, you are only teaching them that grabbing is OK. But you don't want to let them run wild with the item. One way to handle this situation is to hold out your open hand, put a friendly smile on your face, and wait patiently for them to give it back to you. Make sure you don't say *anything*. If they refuse to give it to you, softly stroke their hand or their face. It usually works like a charm. You would not use this method if they had a knife or other dangerous item.

What if your toddler runs off with the item? Toddlers love to be chased. During a fun time, explain to your little one that you two will have chase-me times and non–chase-me times. Then tell the toddler that if you say, "This is not a chase-me time," the toddler must stop what he or she is doing. To reinforce this, role-play both chase-me times and non–chase-me times.

Has your teen been abducted by an electronic device? The tool of holding out your hand works wonders here too. However, you must put a friendly look on your face, and *do not say a word*.

## *Use Loving Guidance*

When parents need their young children to move, some parents guide them from the back of their heads, which throws them off balance, causing them to naturally want to resist. Some parents pull their arms, and this frequently hurts them. The best way to move them is by gently rubbing the small of their back while using gentle forward-moving pressure.

You can use this method with older children too. For example, if you have asked your son to come to dinner and he is not budging from the TV, gently rub and put slight pressure on the middle of his back—*without saying a word*! He may try to bait you with, "Mom, what are you doing?" You can say one word: "Dinner."

• Where could you use loving guidance instead of force?

## *Appeal to Children's Desire to Be Helpful*

Most humans love to be helpful. When locked into a power struggle, we often don't think about asking for our children's help. It feels counterintuitive.

As Mom got out of the car, three-year-old Nathan hopped over the front seat and crawled under the steering wheel, refusing to get out of the vehicle. Mom tried cajoling him at first, then commanding. Finally she threatened him, "If you don't come out now, you won't get to watch your favorite cartoon this afternoon!" None of this worked, as Nathan continued to sit stubbornly underneath the steering wheel.

Mom was about to give up when she remembered to ask for his help. So she said, "Nathan, would you carry the backpack in? My hands are full, and I really need your help." Nathan jumped up immediately at the opportunity to be helpful.

Mastering the skill of getting out and staying out of power struggles has many benefits. You will:

- Feel more in control of the way you react.
- Be an available person to approach.
- Have more respect from your children.
- Gain more cooperation from others.
- Model effective behavior for your children.
- Have more fun being creative in solving problems.
- Experience more synergy with others.
- Have kids who will want to share more of their lives with you.
- Build your character.
- Feel more calm and confident.
- Raise children who will use nonviolent forms of communication.

Not all these methods will work *all* the time. One day something will work like magic, and the next day it won't. But tomorrow it will. The trick here is not to give up when it doesn't work. It takes time, patience, and practice to change old habits.

In addition, you perhaps noticed that one tool is to negotiate while another is to not cave. You are the parent and parents know best. A general rule is if you have been too controlling in the past, you can work on being more flexible. If you have been too "nice," you will want to work on being firmer. As you practice these methods, you will get better and better at knowing what to do when.

Power struggles are prominent in most families. Remember that your children are struggling for independence, power, and influence.

They are not struggling against you. Learn to fight for your children, not against them.

## Temper Tantrums

It is normal for toddlers to have temper tantrums. Neither the part of the brain that controls their impulses nor their vocabulary is fully developed at this stage.

Take care to handle your child gently during a tantrum, both physically and emotionally. Avoid punishing or threatening, arguing, or debating, and dealing with the tantrum in public. Move to a more private place (a restroom, for example) if your child throws a tantrum out in public. Publicly handling temper tantrums is usually embarrassing for both you and your youngster.

Toddlers have temper tantrums for several reasons. They may have a basic need that isn't being met, or they may be struggling for independence, testing limits, or simply feeling frustrated. They communicate with the parent through a tantrum when they don't know any other way.

One of the pitfalls in dealing with tantrums is that they conflict with our need to have things under control. We get angry with our children, and we want to quiet them as quickly as possible. When we simply shush toddlers, we are actually preventing them from developing their brain functions properly. They need us to help them learn how to self-regulate and work through frustration. They need us to take the time to figure out why they are having a tantrum so that we can meet their needs.

When you understand your children's signals, you can take effective action. You can't negotiate with children who are hungry, tired, ill, or hypersensitive. In those cases, get them what they need as quickly as possible.

*It's important to remember that often, in those difficult moments, our child is not simply giving us a hard time—rather, she is having a hard time and needs our help to re-integrate her brain.*

—DANIEL J. SIEGEL AND TINA PAYNE BRYSON, *THE WHOLE-BRAIN CHILD*

There are two very distinct types of tantrums for you to be aware of: a distress tantrum and a tyrant tantrum. It is important to be able to identify which one you are dealing with so you can effectively redirect it.

Here is how to do that.

## Distress Tantrum

You will notice that toddlers can't talk about their feelings or listen to reason. You see real anguish and tears on their face. They are in emotional pain. They seem to be saying, "I can't handle these Big emotions!"

You feel sympathetic.

**Here is what is happening in the brain:**

- Distress tantrums happen because essential brain pathways between children's higher brain and their lower brain haven't developed yet.
- They are experiencing huge hormonal storms in the brain and body.

**Here is what helps:**

- Take the distress seriously.
- Help soothe the child's pain of loss, frustration, and disappointment with understanding and empathy.
- Distract with a game or song.
- Hold the child tenderly (being next to your *calm* body brings the child's overaroused body and brain systems back into balance and releases the calming hormone oxytocin).
- Say, "I know, I know!" rather than phrases to get the child to stop crying.

Helping them emotionally regulate during tantrums enables them to establish brain pathways for managing stress and being assertive later in life.

## *Tyrant Tantrum*

You will notice that there is usually an absence of tears. Toddlers can articulate to demand their way. They may argue, sass, threaten, hit, or kick. These toddlers seem to be saying, "Give me what I want NOW!"

You feel tested or worked.

Tyrant-tantrum toddlers do not experience or show the anguish, desperation, and panic that characterize the distress tantrum. And they don't have stress chemicals flooding their brain and body. It is more about the desire to control or manipulate. They have somehow learned that they can get what they want by screaming, arguing, and threatening.

**Here is what helps:**

- Be firm; don't give in but don't punish.
- Don't negotiate or engage.
- Withdraw attention.
- Ask yourself, "Is there enough parent-child play in your house?"
- Ask yourself, "How can I give this child appropriate power when he or she is not acting inappropriately?"
- Set clear limits and follow through.

If you try negotiating with the tyrant tantrum, you may lose the child's respect. He or she is usually testing you to see if you really mean what you say.

This chart will help you figure out what your child is communicating and what your most effective action will be.

# TEMPER TANTRUM CHART

| Type | What to Do | Example |
|---|---|---|
| **Fatigue** | • Meet child's need.<br>• Minimize all talking that may lead to conflict.<br>• Hold or rock child. | • Take child to bed or a quiet area to rest as soon as you can. |
| **Hunger** | • Meet child's need.<br>• Minimize all talking that may lead to conflict. | • Give child something to eat as soon as possible, even if it's not a scheduled time for a snack or meal. |
| **Illness** | • Meet child's need.<br>• Minimize all talking that may lead to conflict.<br>• Hold or rock child. | • Give child medical assistance if needed. |
| **Hypersensitive** (e.g., clothes, food, abrupt changes) | • Remove object causing reaction as quickly as possible.<br>• Minimize all talking that may lead to conflict. | • If your child's shoe is too tight, loosen it quickly. If it's a garment, take it off. Sometimes children are sensitive to anything scratchy, like rough textures or labels on clothes.<br>• If child is sensitive to abrupt changes, give advance warning or a choice. ("Tommy, we'll be leaving in ten minutes" or "Would you like to leave in seven minutes or ten minutes?") |
| **Testing** | • Do not give in.<br>• Bring child to self-quieting place.<br>• Leave the room.<br>• Do the unexpected. | • There are nonnegotiable boundaries that you have set, and your child is testing your limits. You can discern this type of temper tantrum because you feel manipulated. |
| **Feels Powerless** | • Refuse to negotiate until child is calm and respectful.<br>• Acknowledge anger.<br>• Do win-win negotiation.<br>• Brainstorm solutions.<br>• Give child a sense of power.<br>• If negotiation isn't possible, fantasize with child about his or her unfilled desire. | • "When you calm down, I will be willing to discuss this with you" or "Please use your negotiating voice."<br>• "I understand that you are angry about . . ."<br>• "I want you to win, and I would like to win too. How could we work this out so we can both win?"<br>• Together, write on a sheet of paper all possible solutions.<br>• Ask yourself, "How can I give my child more power in an appropriate way right now?"<br>• "Yes, I would like ice cream too. If you could have some, what kind would you have?" |
| **Frustration** (child is feeling overwhelmed with the task at hand) | • Check your expectations. Are they too high?<br>• Break tasks down into manageable steps.<br>• Make sure child knows how to follow the directions. | • If your child is having a difficult time getting homework done, break it down into ten-minute segments of homework followed by five minutes of play. Repeat cycle until homework is finished. Set a timer for each segment to make process easy to follow. |

# 11

# Redirecting the Mistaken Goal of Revenge

**W**hen children feel overpowered or hurt, either physically or mentally, they become discouraged and resort to the goal of revenge. Feeling worthless, disliked, and hurt by others, these children want to hurt back in the same way they feel they've been hurt.

You may not be the source of the hurt. They may be feeling overpowered by a sibling or bullied by someone at school. Or these children may have a physical limitation, learning challenge, or chronic illness for which they feel angry. The feelings of lack of control or being different from others often generate feelings of revenge. Children who have not bonded well with their parents sometimes seek revenge.

As with other goals of misbehavior, use your own feelings as your guide to your children's intent. When you feel hurt or when you want to hurt your children back, it's a good indication that their goal is revenge for some hurt they have suffered.

If your children have the goal of revenge, they might get bad grades in school, say hateful things, lie, steal, do drugs, mentally or physically abuse siblings, or do anything else to inflict pain.

Ten-year-old Terri got caught stealing fifty cents from a boy at school, and the teacher sent a note to her parents. Terri's mother was livid. "Terri, how could you do this? We would have given you the money.

You have given us nothing but trouble. I just don't understand you. You go to your room. I don't want to see or hear from you until you're sorry for what you've done." Mom gave her a swat on her bottom and sent Terri to her room.

Later that evening, Terri decided to paint her fingernails even though Mom had told her not to play with her mother's nail polish. As Terri was finishing her nails, she "accidentally" spilled the nail polish remover all over Mom's antique table, taking the finish off.

It takes patience and understanding to see behind your children's hurtfulness. It might help to know that sometimes their hatefulness reflects their own feelings about themselves.

If your child is seeking revenge, decide that you will be the first one to stop hurting back. This is difficult to do because we feel justified in wanting to hurt back or in wanting to teach the child a lesson. But ask yourself whether you want peace or war. If you decide you're unwilling to quit the war just yet, that's OK. Just realize that your attempts to discipline will be increasingly less effective.

If you choose peace, take these five steps to redirect the goal of revenge:

**1. Make every attempt to find the source of your child's pain and alleviate it if possible.** If someone or something else is causing your child pain, give the child the help and resources he or she needs. He or she may need a therapist or additional help with homework, and so on.

If you are hurting your child, stop all hurtful actions, words, and punishment. If we retaliate, even though we may temporarily subdue our child's misbehavior, we will only aggravate the problem. Punishment gives the child justification for continued aggression—either direct or indirect.

**2. List five things you love about your child.** You may find it difficult to think about things you love about the child who is hurting you. It is almost impossible to think of creative solutions to problems when you are angry.

**3. Protect yourself from getting hurt.** Sometimes we stay in a situation that is hurtful, hoping that things will get better. However, staying in the presence of abuse usually results in bitterness, resentfulness, hopelessness, and sometimes physical injury.

A sixteen-year-old boy specialized in directing frequent obscenities at his mother. Usually, she would try to make him stop talking to her like that, and that only escalated the problem. She decided to protect herself by leaving the room when she had the slightest inclination he was going to start.

**4. Make amends with the child.** It can be difficult to admit you were wrong or to say you're sorry. We want to wait until the other person apologizes or admits to being wrong first. Remember, you're the adult in this situation and your child is learning about relationships from you. Model the behavior you wish your child to learn.

**5. Reestablish a loving relationship with your child.** Do something to repair the relationship. Go on a date; do something fun together. The purpose is for you to get close again. Do not buy your child things to assuage your guilt.

Your child may be so mad at you that he or she won't allow you to make amends or repair your relationship. This child may need more time to know that he or she can trust your new intentions.

Terri's mother from the previous example recognized that she had hurt Terri and made her feel unloved. Mom tried to make nice, only to be rebuffed by Terri. Mom said nothing about the damaged table. She avoided hurting or punishing Terri further. She also spent time thinking about things she enjoyed about her daughter and mentioned them to Terri. After a two-day cooling-off period, Mom talked to Terri about the incident. "I must have hurt you when I said that you were nothing but trouble. Sometimes I say hurtful things when I don't know what else to do. I'm sorry." Terri softened and said she was sorry for ruining the table. Mom wanted to further rebuild the relationship and suggested, "I've decided to make a centerpiece to cover the spot on the table. Would you like to help me make it?"

Because of the mother's understanding and her determination to end the battle, they were able to enjoy each other's company again.

Teenage Aaron was supposed to be studying. Instead, he was painting a banner for an after-school club. This was a source of irritation to his mother because she had been in an ongoing battle with him about homework since school began. Mom started nagging her son. "You promised you'd do your homework before you did anything else. How come you aren't keeping your word?"

Aaron didn't even bother looking up from the banner. "I will. Now will you quit bugging me?"

His mother gave a sarcastic laugh. "Yeah, I've heard that one before. I want you to stop what you're doing now and finish your homework. You'll never amount to anything!"

Her son stood up and threw the brush down on the banner, ruining it, and shouted, "Why don't you just leave me alone, you @*#? I'll do my homework when I'm ready. I'm sick of you telling me what to do!" He stormed into his bedroom and slammed the door.

His mother realized Aaron was feeling hurt by her and was getting even with her. She decided to be the first of the two to stop the battle. First, she remembered the step of doing something to reestablish their relationship. She let the situation cool down, and later asked him to come out of his room. She offered to help him paint the banner and he agreed. They talked together freely for the first time in months. The next morning, Aaron got up early and finished his homework.

Here are two exercises you can do if you have a particularly difficult child. The first thing is to visualize how you want the relationship to be. Take five minutes in the morning before you start your day and five minutes at night before you fall asleep to visualize your relationship the way you wish it could be. See the images and hear the words that you want each of you to say. Create the feeling you would like to have when the two of you are together.

Parents often imagine the worst possible outcomes for their children—the son gets in an accident, or the daughter uses drugs, and so on. Instead of imagining these possibilities, imagine the possibilities you would most like to see. You may or may not achieve immediate success in visualizing, but be patient.

The second thing you can do with a difficult child is to practice loving them unconditionally. Remember how when they were little, it was even OK if they threw up on your brand-new clothes and you loved them anyway! Try practicing loving them unconditionally for a day. If a day is too long, practice for an hour a day.

Here is an example of a mom who continued to love her daughter through a rough time:

> Halfway through her senior year in high school, Tracy decided to leave home and live in an apartment because her relationship with her mother was so disturbed. Her mother gave her a credit card with the understanding that Tracy would be responsible for paying the bills. Mom got a call from the credit card company because the card was in arrears. Mom was furious that Tracy had been so irresponsible.
>
> It was almost Christmas and Mom was really tempted to punish her daughter and not give her any presents. However, Mom knew she would not teach her daughter anything and would only further alienate her.
>
> Mom paid the card off and cancelled it. Then she made arrangements for Tracy to pay her back.

Mom did four important things: First, Mom stayed unconditionally loving. Second, Mom did not punish her daughter by not giving her presents. Third, Mom canceled the card, sending a message that Tracy could no longer abuse her. The fourth important thing Mom did was to hold Tracy accountable for her actions by arranging for Tracy to pay her back.

Here is an example of how a mother dealt with revenge directed at her even though she was not the source of the child's desire for revenge:

Nathan started yelling, seemingly for no reason, at his mother when she requested something from him. Mom asked, "Did I do something to hurt you?" After lengthy conversation, she found out that Nathan was letting a friend of his intimidate him. Nathan tended to be unassertive and not very self-confident. He and his mother decided to enroll him in an aikido class. Gradually, his self-confidence improved, and the bullying stopped.

Mom located the source of her son's anger and got him the help he needed.

The following two examples are of situations in which the parent and child became extremely entrenched in the pattern of revenge:

Alexa, fifteen, kept destroying her things. She would rip things off her walls and dump her drawers on the floor. Her clothes were often torn and untidy. She and her mother rarely talked. And when her mother would attempt to talk to her, Alexa would roll her eyes in disgust, give her monosyllabic responses, or mumble obscenities under her breath. Mother had often demeaned her and punished her harshly by taking way her privileges and unreasonably grounding her.

During our parenting class, Mom realized her daughter was seeking revenge against her. Mom was determined to alter their relationship. She told Alexa through the door, "I get why you're so angry with me. I've been taking this course to learn how to be a better parent for you. I apologize for how meanly I've been treating you, and I would like to start over if you would be willing to give me a second chance." There was only deafening silence. Mom continued, "I'll wait out here for twenty minutes every afternoon at five o'clock so we can start over. If you want to talk, open the door." Finally, after eleven days, the daughter gingerly opened the door ever so slightly. They had their first short but civil conversation. Mom continued the five o'clock ritual. Each day Mom found the door to Alexa's room open a little bit wider. Three weeks later they were having meaningful conversations and laughing again.

Children who destroy their things feel worthless. They are trying to make their external world match their internal reality. Children with this goal often feel bad, unlovable, and unwanted.

Redirecting this goal when the relationship has become steeped in revenge requires time, patience, and commitment to do doing things differently—and resilience when setbacks occur.

The following is an example of another tenacious mother.

> Mom had a teenage daughter who was so angry with the way Mom had treated her that she wouldn't talk to her. So Mom decided to put Post-it notes on her door with words of encouragement written on them. Every afternoon she would watch her daughter come home and rip the Post-it notes off her door as she slammed it. For twenty-eight days Mom continued unfailingly to write the notes. One day her daughter forgot to bring her gym shoes to school and called Mom to ask her to bring them. As Mom opened her closet door, she noticed that all her Post-it notes were neatly organized in rows on the inside of the closet door.
>
> There was hope!

When you recognize the goal of revenge, use only natural consequences until you establish a better relationship. A child who is looking for an excuse to get even may easily misinterpret a logical consequence as punishment.

Apathy is another sign of revenge. Through this attitude children are saying, "You can't hurt me. I just won't care."

In more extreme cases of revenge, it's important that the whole family see a therapist or counselor. If you send only the child, the child may feel he or she is the problem, and it may only reinforce the child's already negatively skewed picture of him- or herself.

If your child is violent, you may want to see a psychiatrist who can do a brain scan.

A nine-year-old boy viciously attacked a little girl on the playground. He drew pictures of hanging himself and shooting people. The parents had taken him to several therapists and psychiatrists. He had been put on medication. Nothing was working. He went to a psychiatrist who did brain scans and found he had a golf-ball-sized cyst in his brain. It was removed and the boy stopped demonstrating violent tendencies.

Acts of violence or threats of violence must always be taken seriously.

# 12

# Redirecting the Mistaken Goal of Avoidance

**C**hildren who feel like they can't do anything right resort to avoidance, whether the task is easy or challenging. This goal usually appears when everything has been done for these children, so they lack confidence. It also occurs when children have been abused mentally or physically. They don't want to be noticed for fear something bad will happen. Other children use this goal if authority figures are too demanding of them or are high achievers.

Of course, handle any abuse with the proper authorities and therapists.

> Angie's parents had noticed that she was withdrawing more and more from family activities. Her tone of voice was becoming whiny, and she would start crying with the slightest provocation. When asked to participate in activities, she would frequently whimper, "I can't." She also started mumbling words so that it was difficult to understand her. Her parents became extremely concerned about her behavior at home and at school.

Angie began displaying the goal of avoidance. She had become so discouraged that she was giving up. It was as if she was saying, "I'm helpless and useless. Don't make any demands on me. Leave me alone." Children with this goal exaggerate their weaknesses, and they frequently convince us that they are dumb or clumsy. Our initial reaction or response may be to feel sorry for them. You may feel so bad for them that you finish the thing you asked them to do. You rarely reprimand this child. At times you might feel frustrated because nothing seems to work. Some parents react with irritation rather than sympathy to their child's helplessness.

Here are the steps to redirect this behavior.

**1. Stop feeling that these children are not capable.** Do not feel sorry for them, coax them, or make fewer demands on them than you do on other children. When we feel sorry for our children, we encourage self-pity and convince them that we don't have faith in them, that we agree with their belief about themselves. If we help children do something we know they can do for themselves, we encourage this behavior.

**2. Start changing your expectations about your children.** Concentrate on what they have accomplished. Start seeing them as capable. Talk about what they can do; don't discuss what they haven't done.

**3. Be understanding but don't feel sorry for them.** For example, "This feels hard for you" versus "Here, let me do that for you. It's too hard for you, isn't it?"

**4. Make their helplessness inappropriate.** Suppose they say they can't do something that you know they can do. Say to them lovingly, "Do it anyway." Or kiss their cheek and whisper sweetly, "I know you can!" and walk away so that you don't get engaged.

**5. Arrange situations or activities in which children can succeed.** Start with easy things you know they can do and gradually increase the difficulty of the activities as their confidence increases.

> Eight-year-old Liz avoided her schoolwork. Long after a math assignment had been given, the teacher noticed that Liz had not even started the assignment. The teacher asked Liz why. Liz replied meekly, "I can't."
>
> The teacher asked, "What part of the assignment would you be willing to do?"

Liz shrugged.

The teacher asked, "Would you be willing to write your name?" Liz agreed and the teacher left for a few moments.

Liz wrote her name but nothing else. The teacher then asked Liz if she would be willing to do the next two problems, and Liz agreed. This continued until Liz had completed most of the assignment. The teacher had arranged for small successes for Liz by breaking the assignment down into manageable tasks.

Here is an example of how a father encouraged his son with his homework:

Kevin, a nine-year-old boy, was given the assignment of looking up spelling words in the dictionary and then writing out the meanings. His father noticed that Kevin did all he could to avoid his homework. He cried and whined and told his father that he felt stupid. Dad realized that Kevin felt overwhelmed by the project and was defeating himself before he even tried. So Dad decided to break the task down into something that was more manageable for Kevin.

For the first three weeks, Dad looked up the words and Kevin wrote down the meanings. Then Dad also had Kevin look up the first letter of the word in the dictionary. Dad then alternated looking up every other word with Kevin. Dad continued to break down the task until Kevin could successfully do the whole task without his help. The process took several months to complete. It proved to be very helpful to Kevin in his schoolwork and in his relationship with his dad.

Be sincere about all encouragement you offer children who feel defeated and inadequate. These kids are extremely sensitive and suspicious of encouragement and may try to discount it.

## Practice Identifying Goals of Misbehavior

Read the examples, then answer the four questions that follow each one. The answers are on page 174.

**A:** Mary starts tapping her pencil on her desk. The teacher asks her to stop, but the tapping continues. The teacher snaps at Mary, "I said to stop that!"

Mary retorts, "No, I won't, and you can't make me!"

1. How does the teacher feel?
2. What is Mary's reaction to her reprimand?
3. What does Mary's behavior seem to be saying?
4. What would you guess is Mary's goal?

**B:** Mary starts tapping her pencil during class. The teacher says, "Mary." Mary stops immediately and says, "I'm sorry, teacher. Do you want me to say all the ABC's now?"

"Not now, Mary," the teacher responds. "Wait until your turn."

"But I know all of them. Please, can I say them?"

"Well, all right," concedes the teacher.

"Aaa . . . bee . . . cee . . ." Mary's teacher sighs and rolls her eyes as Mary slowly says the alphabet.

1. How does the teacher feel?
2. What is Mary's reaction to her reprimand?
3. What does Mary's behavior seem to be saying?
4. What would you guess is Mary's goal?

**C:** During class, Mary suddenly slams her hand down on the desk and jumps to her feet, saying, "This is stupid going over the ABC's. I learned them a long time ago!"

The teacher is shocked. She responds by curtly telling Mary, "I'll not have you talking to me that way, young lady. I'm sending a note home to your mother."

"Big deal," Mary retorts.

"That does it!" says the teacher sharply. "You're going down to the principal's office!"

1. How does the teacher feel?
2. What is Mary's reaction to her reprimand?
3. What does Mary's behavior seem to be saying?
4. What would you guess is Mary's goal?

**D:** During class, the teacher calls on Mary to say the alphabet. Mary says, "I don't know it," and looks down at her feet.

"Come on now, Mary," the teacher coaxes. "I know you can say it." Mary shrugs. The teacher sighs, then in a gentle voice says, "Come on, Mary, can you say the first letter? Can you say A?"

Mary says weakly, "A?"

"That's good, Mary," the teacher praises.

1. How does the teacher feel?
2. What is Mary's reaction to her reprimand?
3. What does Mary's behavior seem to be saying?
4. What would you guess is Mary's goal?

## Answers

**A**

1. The teacher feels angry. Her authority has been challenged.
2. The reprimand is ignored.
3. "You can't make me."
4. Power.

**B**

1. The teacher feels annoyed.
2. The misbehavior stops because the child received attention.
3. "Notice me."
4. Attention.

**C**

1. The teacher feels hurt and revengeful. Feels like hurting back.
2. Mary hurts the teacher again after the reprimand.
3. "I want to hurt others the way I feel hurt."
4. Revenge.

**D**

1. The teacher feels annoyed and sympathetic.
2. No reprimand is given.
3. "Leave me alone."
4. Avoidance.

One final note on the mistaken goals: these four goals become a concern only when a child becomes embedded in the goal, when the child demonstrates this behavior consistently. Even parents dip into these goals on occasion.

# 13

# Discipline That Gets Results

## Work on One Problem at a Time

It's important to work on one problem at a time so that you and your child don't become overwhelmed or discouraged. After you achieve success with one problem, then move on to the next. For example, achieve success with children making their bed, and then work on cleaning their room.

## Balance Firmness and Kindness

One key to effectiveness is a balance of firmness and kindness. Being kind shows respect for the child. Being firm shows respect for yourself. Being kind and firm demonstrates mutual respect. Some parents are too kind (permissive) and some are too firm (autocratic). Some are both kind and firm, but not at the same time. They put up with a behavior too long and then clamp down on the child. Sound familiar? What works is to combine both qualities in each interaction.

You combine kindness and firmness when you:
- Accept and love your children as they are.
- Do not make your children suffer.
- Do not rescue them from uncomfortable situations they create for themselves.

- Do not allow them to infringe on your rights.
- Take action when misbehavior persists.

> Mom had given Evan a ten-minute heads-up before dinner. However, when the ten minutes were up and Mom called out that dinner was ready, Evan didn't budge from the TV.
>
> Mom moved in close to Evan, knelt down to his level, and asked, "Would you like to turn off the TV or would you like me to?" Again, no response from Evan. So Mom turned off the TV.
>
> "Mommmm," Evan protested.
>
> Mom said nothing as she walked into the dining room.

Parents either give in or get angry when children begin to complain. It is important that you neither argue nor explain, provided they know the reason for your request. If you argue, you are initiating a power struggle; if you explain, you are giving them negative attention. Instead, give your children a look of acceptance and say nothing.

Mom was being kind by giving her son a ten-minute heads-up and by getting down to his level. She was being firm by turning off the TV without repeating herself.

## Talk About Your Problem, Not the Child's

This approach makes your children feel less defensive because you aren't sticking your nose in their business. Say, "I'm unwilling to have a messy living room" instead of, "How many times do I have to tell you to pick up your things?" Here is an experience I had with my husband that makes this point clearer:

> My husband was sitting in the living room reading. I had gone to bed. After a few minutes, I called out to him, "Honey, you have to get up early in the morning, so you'd better not stay up too long."
>
> He answered, "OK, OK," his tone of voice revealing that he didn't appreciate my nagging. About fifteen minutes later, I asked, "Are you going to read much longer?"

He snapped back at me, saying, "I don't know how long I'm going to read!" At that point, he was determined to read all night!

I changed my approach. Instead of sticking my nose into his business, I talked about my problem. I said, "I have to get up early tomorrow, and when you come to bed late, it wakes me up. Would you be willing to come to bed now and read in bed, or would you be willing to sleep in the guest room when you're finished reading?" He reacted quite differently.

He said, "It's not so important that I read right now. I'll come to bed."

Adults and kids alike get irritated when we stick our nose in their business.

Here are two examples that show how most of us have been accustomed to speaking to our children, or how our parents spoke to us. Following each statement is a suggested alternative.

| Old | New |
|---|---|
| "I don't want you watching television until all hours of the evening." | "After 9:00 PM I would like the living room to myself." |
| "Stop that fighting right now! You'll get hurt." | "I'm unwilling to risk damage to my things by allowing you to fight in the house. Go outside if you want to fight." |

Before you start to talk, ask yourself, "What is my problem in this situation?"

Remember that you are addressing *your* problem.

## Ask Questions Instead of Giving Commands

Pretend you are a child for a moment. How would you feel if you heard these commands every day? "Get up! I said, get up! Get dressed! Eat your breakfast! Put your dishes away! No, put that iPad down. Brush your teeth! Come here! Wash your face! Brush your hair! Hurry up, you're making us late!" How are you starting to feel? Maybe irritated, angry, or bossed around? With such a constant harangue, wouldn't you stop listening?

Research tells us that children receive over 232 compliance requests a day from their parents, teachers, and other adults. Imagine if your boss spoke that way to you. My guess is you would quickly be looking for a new job. Fortunately, our children can't go looking for a new family. Nor can they always express how they feel verbally, so feelings show up in their behavior. When we make commands, our children become resistant and often lose initiative because they are waiting to be told what to do. Passive-aggressive behavior is frequently an outcome of being told what to do. Children resist, dawdle, or forget; sometimes they put their hands over their ears to shut us out physically. And more important, they don't have to think.

Here are some samples of questions you can ask:
- What's happening?
- Where do your shoes belong?
- What is next on your schedule?
- What is one thing you can do to help?
- What's your plan?
- What do you need in order to get that done?
- How can I help?
- What needs to get done before we _____ ?
- How could you say that more respectfully?
- Was that helpful or hurtful?

Here is an idea for youngsters. Together make a list of everything they need to get done before they leave for school. Put the activities on a note card, one per card. Help them to put the cards in the order in which they need to happen. Put them in horizontal order and then hold them together with a brightly colored ribbon and glue. Hang the activities on the back of their door or someplace convenient to them. Then instead of saying, "Brush your teeth!" you can ask, "What's next on your activity board?"

Instead of putting the words on the note cards, you can take pictures of your child doing the activity and paste them onto the cards. Or you can cut out pictures of the activities and paste them on the note cards.

Asking questions instead of barking orders develops:

- Judgment skills.
- Consequence skills.
- Accountability skills.
- Initiative skills.
- Problem-solving skills.
- Cooperation skills.

## Concentrate on What You Can Do

During conflicts, most of us concentrate and talk about what the other person should do instead of thinking about what we can do. Stop and ask yourself, "What can I do?" By controlling your own actions rather than trying to control someone else's, you can influence the other person's behavior without disturbing the relationship.

Instead of talking too much, take friendly action. Give children their comb or their toothbrush with toothpaste on it. Guide children to their task by gently and lovingly placing a hand on their back.

> Mother was tired of nagging and reminding her children to set the table every night. She decided to take some action. That evening, she put the food on the table, sat down, and silently waited. The kids came in and asked, "What are we waiting for, Mom?" At that point, Mother could have lectured, "We wouldn't have to wait if you had done what I've told you to do a hundred times!" Instead, she very briefly and casually answered, "Silverware and plates." The kids rushed off and came back with the silverware and dishes.

> Another mother whose children seldom picked up their dirty clothes without being nagged simply stated, "From now all, I'll only wash clothes that are in the hamper." She then acted by not washing clothes left out of the hamper. Her children understood the message and made sure dirty clothes made it to the hamper.

Both mothers quit nagging and reminding, and this helped them to feel better about themselves and their children. When we spend less time being negative, we can enjoy our children a lot more.

## Children Don't Need to Suffer to Learn

In the past, some parents believed that children needed to suffer if they were to learn. Many of us still believe this, often subconsciously. It affects our tone of voice and gestures when we discipline children. To demonstrate the idea of subconscious beliefs, consider this example.

> A father and his son were in an automobile accident. The father was killed instantly. The boy, who was seriously injured, was rushed to the hospital. A doctor washed up, walked into the operating room, looked at the boy, and exclaimed, "I can't operate on this boy. He's my son!"

How do you explain this? The answer is the doctor was the boy's mother. Our subconscious belief might make us assume the doctor was a man. If I had asked you, "Do you believe all doctors are men?" you would probably have answered, "Of course not." But your subconscious belief, and not your common sense, made you think the doctor was a man.

Likewise, when we discipline children, we often operate from our subconscious belief that children must suffer to learn.

> There was a boy in summer camp whose mother asked for my help. Her son refused to wash his hands before meals. She was quite irritated by this. When the child arrived at camp, I said to him in a friendly tone of voice, "Tom, it's your business if you wash your hands or not, but when you come to the table with dirty hands, you pass germs around. I don't want to get sick. So unless you have a better idea, from now on I will only serve people who come to the table with clean hands."
>
> That very afternoon Tom put me to the test by coming to the table with dirt on his hands. I calmly reached across the table and removed his plate. Do you know what that kid did? He sat right across from me and smiled through the whole meal. I was boiling inside. He appeared not to care that he wasn't eating. Finally, I said gruffly, "You know, you're not getting anything to eat until dinnertime!"

I said the wrong thing. The outcome of his behavior became a punishment. I was now involved in the same power struggle he had with his mother. The thing that got me into trouble was that without being consciously aware of it, I believed that if Tom didn't suffer, he wouldn't learn.

When children see that your intent is not to make them suffer, they'll become more cooperative.

## Choose Closeness Instead of Being Right

Concentrate on developing closeness in your relationship with your children. Don't concern yourself with who is right or wrong. Nobody cares about how much you know. You can google just about anything you want to know. Children do care about your ability to connect with them.

Ask yourself, "Do I want to be right, in control, or close?" Asking this question is helpful in all relationships.

## Teach Self-Quieting

A time-out is a common discipline tool that becomes punishment when a parent uses it in an angry manner and to control children. For example, imagine you heard the words, "I'm sick and tired of your whining! Go to your room and stay there until you can behave!" While you were in your room, would you be thinking: (a) "Wow, I was not acting appropriately. I need to stop whining!" or (b) "This is stupid! I'm angry! Mom isn't fair!" I am assuming you would choose the second option.

Notice that the parent is sending you away in anger. The message you may receive is, "I don't like you. I want you to go away." When parents are in control of when their children come out of their room, children do not learn self-control. When time-out is seen as punishment, children feel resentful. They don't think about what to do differently in the future. Time-out loses its effectiveness when it becomes punishment. Self-quieting, on the other hand, teaches internal control and self-responsibility.

Self-quieting is what you, or your child, can do to get to a peaceful state of mind where you can work through emotions and find solutions to your problem. How old were you when you learned self-quieting? Wouldn't it be great to have had this skill at a very young age?

Parents can be a model for their children that they don't have to whine, complain, or argue, but can instead turn within to find solutions and find an inner sense of calm.

What do you need to self-calm? Here are a few options: Do you need to talk to someone, go for a run, clean the house, or listen to music? Or perhaps you need to meditate. Typically, we all use one or two of the following senses:

1. **Kinesthetic** includes physical movement, such as playing with Play-Do, drawing, water play, pounding on a tool bench, blowing bubbles or a pinwheel, running, or jumping on a trampoline.
2. **Olfactory** includes smelling things like potpourri, something with the mother's scent on it, or child-safe essential oils (lavender is a good one).
3. **Visual** includes reading books, looking at pictures, watching a fish tank or lava lamp, educational screen time, and observing glitter wands.
4. **Auditory** involves listening to peaceful music or nature sounds, a book on tape, or talking through one's feelings with someone.
5. **Lack of stimulus** includes meditation, closing one's eyes, and breathing deeply.

Help children to identify how they like to self-soothe. Then help them to a space where they can go to calm down. You can make a special bag or box for car trips, restaurants, and other public places.

Here are some examples of self-calming spaces:
- One toddler loved to take baths to calm down.
- A teenage boy jumped on his trampoline.

- A girl climbed a tree and stayed there until she calmed down.
- A young boy had his dad put up a pup tent in their family room.
- Another child put several of the items listed above under the staircase in the house.

Create a self-quieting space with your children. This space shouldn't be in their bedroom. It could be in the kitchen, the study, a corner tucked away somewhere, or, weather permitting, outside. Help your children find things to bring to their self-quieting space that help them quiet themselves and work through their feelings.

Children will learn self-quieting most effectively if you model it for them. For the first few times, you might even go to their self-quieting space with them and show them what to do.

One option is to place the following three questions on the wall in their self-quieting space:

- What is the problem?
- What is my part in the problem?
- What is one thing I can do to improve the situation?

The following is a list of things to do when you ask children to take a self-quieting break:

- Get on their level, eye to eye, and speak calmly and lovingly.
- Say to them, "It looks like you need a break. Go to your self-quieting place [or whatever name they have for it]. Come back when you're calm and ready." Say this once, and only once, to your children.
- If children do not leave, pick them up or lead them gently and lovingly to their self-quieting space.
- If children come back and act appropriately, let them stay. If their behavior is not appropriate, take them back to their space without saying a word. You may have to take them to their space several times. Be patient and persistent.

When you tell your children, "Come back when you're ready," you're teaching them to act from an internal sense of control. If you say, "Come out in five minutes," you have decided when they're ready.

When my son was two and a half years old, I had invited some friends over for dinner. At dinner, Tyler started acting inappropriately. I first asked him to stop. He calmed down for a few seconds and then began to act out again. I gently picked him up and took him to his self-quieting space. I said, "You may come back when you're ready."

He came back immediately and continued to act inappropriately. I picked him up and took him out of the room. This time I didn't say a thing. He came in again and acted inappropriately. This time his father took him out. We must have taken him out of the room fourteen times. After the fourteenth time, Tyler sat for a whole hour at the table without being inappropriate.

Couples have an advantage when they agree to use the same discipline methods because they can take turns with a persistent child. You may think, "Fourteen times! Who has the time to do that?" Yes, it took patience to do this the first time, but the more I used the method, the quicker Tyler responded.

You and your partner may want to devise a signal or use a special word with each other when you notice that self-quieting is needed. One family I know uses the peace sign of the 1960s. A preschool calls the self-quieting room the "happy place" because the children go there to collect their thoughts and return to the group in a happy frame of mind. Whether you are a teacher or a parent, it is best to have the children determine the name of their space. When children have ownership, they are more likely to use the space.

If your child's goal is revenge or power, you may get into a battle with him or her about taking a self-quieting break. Stop what you're doing and take the self-quieting break yourself.

## Setting Limits

Limits tell your family under what condition you are willing or unwilling to do something. They signify where you draw the line. They tell people what you will or will not tolerate. The purpose of limits is to take care of you. Limits are not designed to control or manipulate someone else's behavior.

Limits give others important information about you to help them know what they can or cannot expect from you. Limits are about your needs, not about criticizing someone else's behavior or about trying to make him or her act in a certain way.

## Why Do Children Need Limits?

Children need limits so they can learn to recognize and respect other people's limits. Limits provide a sense of security as well. Without them, children feel abandoned and confused, and sometimes they bounce off the walls to find them. Limits help children feel that we care about them. Our teens want limits even though they act like they don't.

Children also need limits to learn how to deal with conflict. What happens when they disregard someone's limits? What happens when someone disrespects the limits they have set? Children need limits to help them define themselves. The limits you set help your children set their own as they watch you model asserting yours.

Limits help children learn what is socially acceptable. They need to learn that if they go past a certain point, there will be consequences. Some may be serious, such as getting in trouble with the law.

## Issues to Set Limits Around

Some common limits you may want to set are limits around the use of your belongings, screen time, bedtime, your time, profanity, mealtime, chores, care and feeding of pets, and use of the car. This is not an exhaustive list by any means. Add to it things that are important in your family.

## Infringement of Limits

The best clue as to whether your limits are being violated is by how you feel. If you feel any of these emotions, your limits are being dishonored, or you have not been clear about them:

- angry
- resentful
- overburdened
- taken advantage of

- abused
- smothered
- unappreciated
- torn between people you love

## *Why Is It Hard to Set Limits?*

Your ability to set limits and follow through is largely determined by how you were parented as a child. Children who had no limits set for them or were unsupervised much of the time grow up not knowing how to set their own limits. Children who suffered put-downs like, "Don't make waves," "Children should be seen and not heard," and "You're being selfish" also have trouble setting limits.

Abuse in homes—mental, physical, emotional, sexual, drug or alcohol, or work—violates limits and keeps people from feeling worthy of setting limits.

Limits are difficult to set in situations where there is serious illness or disability. If self-sacrifice was modeled and expected of you when you were a child, limits are even harder to set as a parent.

Sometimes we don't set limits because we don't know how to set them. Sometimes we feel guilty about our own actions, such as working too much or getting divorced. Fear of conflict prevents some parents from setting limits. Perhaps the child will get angry and reject the parent. Instead of directly setting limits, we often handle problems by:

- Acting or pretending as if nothing happened (denial).
- Ignoring the problem and hoping it will go away.
- Talking ourselves out of our feelings.
- Making excuses for another person's behavior.
- Going over and over the event, trying to make sense of it and paralyzing ourselves in the meantime.
- Blaming ourselves or someone else.
- Hurting the other person.
- Acting like we're above having those feelings.
- Pretending that we don't care.
- Withholding love or communication.

## *Steps for Setting Limits*

1. **Identify the behavior you want to set a limit around.**
2. **Get clear about what you want your outcome to be.** Many behavioral problems can be averted when we have clarity. When we are unclear, children are likely to feel confused and push against our boundaries to get clarity.
3. **Discuss the limit with your child.** You want to make sure your child is apprised of the behavior you expect from him or her.

## *Steps for Implementing Limits*

If children disregard the limit, follow these steps:

1. **Empathize with your children.** Make sure that they feel understood, heard, and accepted. All three of these elements are necessary for effective results. Sometimes this step alone is sufficient. Setting limits works only when there is a relationship. Once you have empathized, pause and wait for their acknowledgment that they feel heard by you.
2. **Use one or two words.** Children often try to negotiate with parents. To prevent this scenario from becoming a debate, just use one word that represents the limit you have set. For example, if the issue is bedtime, just say that one word, *bedtime*.
3. **Offer them a choice.** Choices that are fun are often the most successful, such as, "Would you like to go to bed hopping like a bunny or prancing like a horse?" On the other hand, some choices aren't always fun.

Here is an example of how it works:

Brianna was three when I set the limit that she could have one sugary treat per day if it was before 6:00 PM. We had discovered that if she had sugar after that, she would be up all night partying.

One evening we were at the grocery store. She asked if she could have a glazed doughnut as she looked longingly through the case at its chocolate icing. I almost said, "You can't have any sugar now. You'll be up all night!" Luckily the parenting gods were with me and instead I did the first step in the process of setting limits. "That glazed dough-nut looks like it would really taste good. I can see why you want it."

Then I paused and bit my tongue, so I would not say the word *but*. The word *but* usually negates what you have said prior to it. She nodded at me as if she felt some consolation regarding her desire. Then she pleaded again. I responded with the second step and said, "One sugar."

"Would you like these grapes or would you like an apple?" was the third step, where I gave her a choice.

She chose the apple and chomped merrily on her way.

I think it went that smoothly because she really felt heard, under-stood, and accepted by me. Generally, the degree to which your child feels understood will be the degree of cooperation you get.

Here is an example of implementing these steps around homework:

Justine had homework to do but her friend was knocking at the door enticing her to play. Justine knew that she and her parents had agreed on a set homework time. "Let me go play for just ten minutes," she begged.

Mom said empathetically, "You really like Megan. You have a lot of fun with her."

"Homework," said Mom cheerfully yet somehow firmly at the same time.

"But, Mom." Justine started to rebuff her mother.

"Would you like to start with your math or science?"

Justine, having experienced Mom's resoluteness before, sullenly opened her math book and began to work.

Here is example of a dad and his preschooler:

Ian knew that he had go to preschool. Dad had been preparing him since early that morning by saying things like, "I wonder what you and Micah will do today? Your teacher makes the best snacks, doesn't she?" What Ian really wanted was to stay home with Dad. Dad said wisely, "I hear that you want to stay home with me today. It's hard to be apart."

Ian looked up at Dad, clearly yearning to spend more time with him. "Preschool day," said Dad.

Ian protested loudly.

Dad gave him a choice: "Would you like to walk to the car by yourself or would you like me to carry you?'

Ian, still protesting, refused to budge, so Dad gently picked him up and carried his squirmy, squealing toddler to the car. As soon as Ian calmed down a bit, Dad started talking about what fun they were going to have when Ian got home from preschool later that day.

Be consistent and follow through. It is imperative that you do what you say. When you don't, children learn that parents are all talk and no action. The sooner you act, the sooner your children will recognize their limits. Whenever you give a choice that you don't intend to enforce, you are making an idle threat and reinforcing unwanted behavior.

### *What to Expect When You Begin to Set Limits*

If you are just starting to set limits, expect that your child's behavior will get worse. Children will test you. They will try everything in their power to get you to go back to the way you used to be. Think carefully before you set a limit to be sure you can follow through and enforce it when your child tests it. Remember, it is normal for children to test limits. They are not being brats. Testing limits is their job!

## Consequences

Two types of consequences are useful in disciplining children. One is a natural consequence, where the result of the child's action is whatever happens naturally, without any interference from anyone. The other is a logical consequence, where the parent's response to the child's unwanted behavior makes sense to the child.

## *Use of Natural Consequences*

Ask yourself, "What would happen if I didn't do anything?" That result is a natural consequence. If you act when you don't need to, you strip your child of the chance to experience the natural consequences of his or her actions. Natural consequences are very effective teachers.

You get to eliminate nagging and reminding. The situation itself disciplines your child.

> *Nagging makes it your problem. Silence makes it theirs.*
> —Barbara Coloroso

Mother recognized that her twelve-year-old Jenny had developed a habit of forgetting things. Luckily, Mother had heard the expression "A child who always forgets has a parent who always remembers."

Jenny was making a project for a science class. She was adding the final touches and was supposed to take it to school the next morning. However, Jenny was in a hurry leaving for school and forgot to take the project. Mother noticed that Jenny had forgotten and resisted the temptation to remind her. Instead, she let natural consequences take effect.

Later that day, Mother received a phone call from Jenny asking her to bring the project. Mother told her, in a very friendly tone, "No, Jenny, I'm unwilling to do that," and changed the subject.

This experience gave Jenny a lesson in remembering. Mother would have lessened the learning experience if she had brought the project to Jenny or had said, "See what happens when you forget?" Then Jenny could have focused on Mother's critical comment rather than on her own responsibility to remember. If Jenny did not have a habit of forgetting Mother would have brought her project to school.

Natural consequences are more effective than logical consequences, where you set up the disciplinary action. There are three situations where you would want to use a logical consequence instead of a natural one. They are:

- When the natural consequence would be hazardous to the well-being of your child. For example, a natural consequence of playing in the street is he or she would be hit by a car.
- When the natural consequence interferes with your rights or the rights of others, such as when a teen continues to play music at a loud volume even after he or she has been asked to turn it down.
- When the effects of the natural consequence are too long range for the child to connect cause and effect. For example, the natural consequence for a child who does not brush his or her teeth is cavities.

## Use of Logical Consequences

If self-quieting, setting limits, and natural consequences have not been effective tools to solve a particular problem, you may need to use a logical consequence. Your child must recognize the logic of the discipline for it to be effective. It's a very common mistake for parents to use a consequence that has no relevance to the child's behavior. For example, taking away television privileges for breaking a window is not relevant to the offense. Your child is more likely to feel like he or she is being punished and may then rebel. On the other hand, it would be logical for a child to do chores (such as mow lawns) to help pay for the new windowpane. Your child is not being punished but is instead learning to repair the mistake.

For logical consequences to be effective, they must incorporate the following three Rs of logical consequences. These are: respectful, reasonable, and related.

### Respectful

Always show respect for your children. Allow them as much input as possible into the determination of the consequence. Avoid anything that causes your children to feel guilt or shame so that they don't view the consequence as a punishment.

*Reasonable*

Consequences that are excessive or harsh cause your children to focus on what they perceive as punishment, instead of repairing their mistake. They are likely to react in a revengeful way.

*Related*

The consequence needs to be related to the mistake. If children make a mess, they clean it up. If they hurt someone, they try to ease the pain. If they damage something, they repair or replace it. Remember that punishment results in anger and resentment, while logical consequences teach them to be responsible for their mistakes.

## Logical Consequences Relate to Future Behavior

Logical consequences are set up to improve future behavior, not to punish past behavior. If you are in the middle of a conflict, don't try to develop logical consequences at that time. All you'll be able to think of is a "logical punishment" because you're probably upset. Instead, step out of the conflict and take time to calm down. Then, during a peaceful time, work through the logical consequence's steps that follow and go through the steps with your child.

Notice that this process is the same as the steps for conflict resolution except steps 1 and 7. The reason for thinking of three things you love about your child is that you're probably feeling angry with your child. It's extremely difficult to think of creative solutions when you're angry. The purpose of step 1 is to change your attitude so that you will think of a consequence instead of punishment.

## Logical Consequences Steps

1. List three things you love about your child.

2. Ask your child's permission for a particular time to work out a logical consequence together.

3. Tell your child, "I want . . ." Say what you want to have happen and why, simply and clearly, without guilt, blame, shame, and exaggerations.

4. Ask your child what he or she wants and why. Write that down too.

5. Brainstorm a list of possible solutions with your child on a separate sheet of paper.

6. Create a solution to the problem from the list. Let your child cross off unacceptable solutions first, then you do the same. Choose one suggestion or a combination of suggestions you both agree to and write it down.

7. If you are concerned your child will forget, acknowledge him or her for cooperating. Say, "Thanks for working this out with me. What should I do if you happen to forget?" Now come up with a logical consequence using either your child's suggestion, which works best, or your suggestion. Once you have discussed and agreed on a logical consequence, write it down.

8. After you have used the logical consequence for a designated amount of time, ask yourself, "Did I get results that were good for my child and me? Do I need to improve the logical consequence?" You can start the process all over again if necessary. Sometimes you need to try more than one solution.

Here is an example of how one dad handled bikes left unlocked:

Dad bought his two boys new bikes, helmets, and locks. Neither boy seemed able to get in the habit of locking up his bike despite punishment, rewards, bribes, and threats from the parents, who were at their wit's end.

Dad decided to try a logical consequence instead. He told the boys (when he was feeling calm), "There's a situation I'd like to change. Is this a good time to talk?"

"Yeah," said the boys.

Dad continued, "I've noticed I've been bugging you guys about locking your bikes. That makes you mad, doesn't it?"

The boys looked puzzled and answered with some hesitation, "Yeah . . ."

Dad went on, "I think I've figured out why I have a problem. I realize I gave you the bikes and they're yours. It's not my business if you choose to risk having them stolen. However, I would feel bad. They were expensive, and I'm not willing to buy two more bikes. Do you guys have any ideas about how I can solve my problem?"

The boys told Dad they would lock up the bikes. Dad said, "Thanks, that would solve the problem. What should I do if you forget?" because they usually did.

Both boys replied, "I don't know."

"Well, how about I lock them up if you forget?" asked Dad.

"OK," said the boys.

"We'll try that for a few weeks and see how it works. If you boys think of a better idea, we'll talk about it," said their dad.

A few mornings later, Tom came running into the house shouting, "Somebody chained our bikes to the porch!"

His mom resisted the temptation to explain and instead asked, "Hmmm, I wonder why?"

Five minutes later, Tom came back inside, saying, "I locked my bike now. Would you take the chain off?"

Mom replied in a friendly tone, "Dad has the key and he's at work."

Tom asked, "Will you drive us to school?"

Mom said lovingly, "Sorry, that would make me late to work."

Tom and his brother had to walk a few blocks to school that morning.

When Dad came home and found both boys had locked their bikes, he removed the chain. About two weeks later, the boys forgot again, and Dad chained the bikes to the porch. From that day on, the boys remembered to lock their bikes.

Here is an example of kiddos not cleaning the kitchen:

Our kids had agreed to clean the kitchen before I came home from work, but it wasn't getting done. I called, "Do you guys have a minute?"

"Sure, Mom," said Tyler and Brianna.

"I have something I'd like to change. I've been nagging you a lot lately about not keeping your agreement to clean the kitchen. I'll bet you are tired of it," I said empathetically.

They answered quizzically, "Yeah?"

I continued, "I'm not willing to cook in a dirty kitchen because I don't want to do all the work. What do you think I could do?"

They both mumbled in their own way, "I don't know."

I suggested, "Well, how about I try this? I don't want to be nagging you anymore nor do I want to cook in a messy kitchen. You can choose to clean kitchen or not. If by 5:00 PM you haven't cleaned the kitchen, then I'll do it instead of cooking dinner. Is that OK with you?"

They chimed, "Oh, Mom, we'll clean the kitchen."

"Thanks a lot, that will help me. What should I do if you forget? We all forget sometimes," I asked.

"We won't forget," they promised.

"I'm unwilling to do nothing. How about we try what I've suggested? If you think of a different plan, let me know," I said.

The kitchen was cleaned for a few days and then they "forgot." I cleaned the kitchen that night instead of making dinner. I had to do this several times over the course of the month.

Notice that in both examples, the consequence involved some action the parent could take. It did not involve trying to make the child do something. We can control what we do. We can't control what others do.

If you create a logical consequence and discover that it isn't working, and maybe the problem has worsened, then perhaps you really are using punishment.

### What Children May Say

Parents can increase the likelihood of working out effective, logical consequences when they know how to handle kids' responses to the process. Children may say, "I don't know" when asked for ideas. You can say, "Then how about we try this . . . and if you think of a different plan, let me know." Some children may want a solution you don't like. If so, say, "I'm unwilling to do that. Do you have another suggestion?"

If your children have been accustomed to punishment, they may say, "You can spank me," or some other form of punishment. I recommend you say, "I'm unwilling to hurt you. What else do you suggest?" Don't be fooled into thinking that if they select a punishment, that makes it OK.

If they promise that they will not repeat the offense or mistake and they're not good at keeping their word, say, "Thanks. That will make things better for me. What would you like me to do if you break this agreement?"

If your children suggest a reasonable consequence and you agree to it, say, "I'll try that for a week. Thanks."

## *Applied Logical Consequences*

It is sometimes expedient for a parent to apply a logical consequence without going through the planning process and using a worksheet. When you apply a logical consequence, you do something that is logically related to your child's behavior. For example, if your child spills his or her milk, you hand over a dishrag.

> Mom was continually nagging her two children to unroll their dirty socks before they put them in the clothes hamper. She decided to try a logical consequence. She simply didn't wash socks that were rolled up. After two weeks, all the rolled-up socks were still in the hamper and Mom said nothing. A few days later she noticed that all the socks were still in the hamper, but someone had unrolled them. Both kids became diligent about unrolling their socks, and a word was never spoken. Mom didn't have to remind them, and the kids didn't feel nagged.

## Summary of Consequences

### *Natural Consequences*

A natural consequence flows out of events. The parent does not do anything to interfere, arrange, or impose.

## *Logical Consequences*

The parent and child meet to decide on a mutually agreeable solution to a problem. The consequence is logically related to the child's behavior. Logical consequences are used when a good relationship exists between the parent and child.

## *Applied Logical Consequences*

The parent makes an impromptu decision without discussing the situation with the child. The consequence is logically related to the child's behavior and is applied.

# Eight Steps for Correction

These steps are a gentler approach to discipline and teach more life skills. I recommend it over logical consequences.

1. Wait until you are both cooled off. This is hard to do but if you talk while you are angry, you may say things you will regret. Your children will most likely get defensive and not learn anything from the exchange.

2. Ask for permission. Make sure that this is a good time to have this important conversation. It also prepares children for a difficult topic, and it shows children respect for their heart and time.

3. Share your observations of the event to be discussed. Use as few words as possible, avoiding blame and shame.

4. Ask children what happened. We often jump to conclusions and make accusations that might not be true. Try to ask the question from a place of curiosity and nonjudgment.

5. Ask them how they feel about what they did again without judgment.

6. Ask children, "How do you think your behavior affected _____?" or "What was the impact of your action?" It could be you, a teacher, a friend, or a sibling. You may be tempted to just tell your children, but it is important to ask them the question. Most children lack the brain development to think about the implications of

the behavior and the effect they have on others. This question teaches them the important life skill of empathy.

7. Invite them to do a make up. This teaches children that when they make a mistake, it is important to repair the relationship by doing something to make up for their error. It teaches them the following essential life skills.

- To be accountable for their actions
- To get back in integrity with themselves
- To restore trust in the relationship

8. Rehearse or role-play the more effective way your children could have handled the situation; do this several times if necessary. You are looking for a response that feels solid rather than insincere or unassertive. If they are younger, adding a story about their situation can help solidify the concept you want them to learn.

Tell children, "I will not punish you or make you feel bad about what you did, but I do want you to practice doing it the effective way so that you can be more successful."

## Results of Discipline

To make sure you are on target with discipline and your children are learning what you wish them to learn, ask yourself these questions:

- What happens to your children after they're disciplined? Are they angry? Do they get back at you overtly or covertly? Are they fully cooperating or are they withdrawn and sullen?
- What happens to their self-esteem? Is it lowered or enhanced?
- Do they feel empowered to repair their mistake?
- Do they become more externally motivated or inspired from within?
- What happens to your relationship? Is communication better? Will they be more or less likely to tell you about their mistakes in the future or will they be too afraid? Did you win the battle (get the child to do what you wanted) and lose the war (dampen your delicate relationship)?

- Does the interaction encourage your children to discuss their wants and feelings? Or do they become hesitant to express their feelings or opinions?
- Does the interaction improve their ability to solve conflicts in a way that allows both of you to win?
- Do they learn about their behavior in a way that provides increased choices? Or do they learn that they have limited choices?

Here is a powerful process that will speed up the process exponentially. Before you go to bed at night, pick one situation (more than one can be overwhelming) where you had an altercation with your child that day. Recall for just a minute, without beating yourself up—it is vital that you are not critical of yourself during this exercise—how it felt for both you and your child. Then think about how you would do it differently if it happened again tomorrow. The final touch is important: Visualize yourself doing it differently and achieving the outcome you want. Add emotions, feeling the warmth of hugging your child, feeling your connection, experiencing your child saying, "I love you!" Get into your emotions as much as possible. This process will help you rewire your brain and start to put new habits in place. If you like to journal, this would be ideal because you can track your progress.

# 14

# "Why Can't They Just Get Along?"

**I**t starts with who gets to use the bathroom first, then someone looks at someone else the wrong way at the breakfast table. The arguing continues as they fight over who gets to lock the front door. For some parents, it feels like the fighting will never end.

While it is true that some sparring can enhance social skills such as negotiation, there are a couple of downsides. Frequent, intensive fighting heightens the risk of anxiety and depression and can lower children's self-esteem. Furthermore, recent research has found that siblings who seriously battle are more likely to engage in delinquent behaviors, including drug use.

Another downside to allowing sibling warfare is that children are forming patterns in their brain on how to deal with conflict for the rest of their lives. We want our children to learn the skills of being a better team player, truly listening to one another, and negotiating. Children who learn how to work together will naturally want to help one another out instead of sabotaging one another. Quarrelsome behavior drains everyone's energy and can try the patience of the most peaceful parent.

Parents often tolerate and accept fighting as inevitable. With all the other problems in our lives, sibling fights don't get the problem-solving attention they deserve. However, when you look globally at what happens when people fight over possessions, territory, philosophies, resources, and race, you see war. We need to practice new ways of being that promote peace, and the place to start is in our families.

It may seem a bit extreme to compare our children's fights to war. However, our children are the future leaders of the world. Wouldn't it be great if they learned win-win negotiation skills in childhood, and then could bring these skills into our governments?

Parents have a tremendous opportunity to contribute to peace by dealing with children's fights in ways that encourage children to learn to solve their differences in a peaceful manner. We need to encourage the values of peacefulness and cooperation. World peace begins in the hearts and homes of our families. When the consciousness changes in our homes, it will change in our governments and our world community as well.

Children can learn numerous nonviolent ways to prevent altercations. Home is a good place to begin learning and practicing these skills with your help.

Below are some reasons children fight:
- To get a parent's attention
- Boredom
- To get a parent to choose one child over another
- To overpower
- For excitement
- To release tension
- To get their way
- To get rescued
- They don't know how to get attention from their sibling appropriately

How can we prevent fighting? First, let's look at some things we do unknowingly to encourage their fights.

**Use comparisons.** "I wish you would get good grades like your sister." Statements like this make children feel resentful toward their sibling.

**Encourage competition.** "Whoever gets to the car first wins!" This seems like an innocent statement. However, it provokes competition and encourages fighting words like, "I get to sit in the front seat. I was here first."

**Tell them not to feel negative feelings toward their sibling.** This is one way we teach our children to be afraid to share their feelings with us. The feelings don't go away; they are likely to intensify because they are never dealt with in a healthy way. Instead of saying, "You don't hate your brother," empathize with your child's anger. Say, "I can understand that you're really angry with Jason right now."

**Force children to share.** Be sure your children have some things they don't have to share. Designate items the whole family can share and items that are personal belongings.

**Rescue.** Rescuing one child from another sets up a victim/bully mentality that is not healthy.

**Have a favored child.** Children are very sensitive to parents who show favoritism. Children get favored for different reasons: being the "baby," being chronically sick, being the "bad" kid, or excelling at an activity that requires a lot of time and attention. Resentment is created when one child gets more attention than another—either positive *or* negative attention.

**Label children.** When children are labeled "good" or "bad," they tend to live up to our expectations. Believe it or not, the "good" child often provokes the "bad" child. The "good" child often tattles on the "bad" one to get him or her into trouble.

## Redirecting Arguments to Peaceful Resolutions

Children need to be taught the skills to negotiate, cooperate, and maintain peace in the home. The following skills are important to teach at the right developmental stage.

### *Tips for Redirecting Fighting with Youngsters*

For little ones who might not have the vocabulary or understanding of negotiation, you can teach them how to trade instead of grab or whine to get what they want. You can also teach them how to use their words.

*Encourage Assertiveness*

Some toddlers are taken advantage of because they don't stand up for themselves; then they become angry. Teach your unassertive youngster to say the words "Stop it!" until the offender backs off. Another technique is for your toddler to hold out his or her hand and loudly say, "My space." Unassertive children often use quiet, whiny voices, so you may have to help your child practice using a strong voice.

*Show How to Take Turns and Trade*

Many problems among siblings arise when both want to use the same toy, or ball, or clothes, or whatever (depending on their ages). Teach children how to take turns or to trade one thing for another. It helps to use an impartial aid like a timer to let children know how long they must wait before they get their turn. Do not force your children to share or give up a toy before they are done with it as it interferes with their sense of completion when they are done.

*Demonstrate Self-Control and Relaxation*

A good place to start learning peaceful ways to solve problems is to teach your kids healthy responses to anger. Teach children to breathe deeply in through the nose and out through the mouth to the count of ten when they feel angry. This will relax them and give them time to think before acting. Model using this technique yourself, and at the same time, express your emotions clearly and calmly.

*Teach Children How to be Kind*

Teach your children to consider each other's feelings. Any solution to a problem often works best if feelings are taken into consideration. You could say, "Micah, tell Megan how you feel when she takes your toy."

*Model Respect and Joy in Play*

Children need to learn how to join others in play in ways that are inviting. Aggressive or whiny children are not welcome playmates. You can use dolls or puppets to role-play with a child who is having trouble learning how to play with others. Let him or her play with two creatures, and you be the third who wants to join the fun. Behave in ways that are not acceptable and talk about what to do differently. Then have your child practice.

### Describe What You See and Empathize

Describe without judgment what you see occurring during the children's fight. When you make them aware of what they're doing, they then can choose if they want to continue. If you speak judgmentally, the children are likely to become defensive. For example, "I see Ezra has the trike and Megan wants a turn."

### Don't Force Your Children to Share

When we force children to share, we don't allow them the opportunity to feel fulfilled by their play and share the toy from an experience of being complete. Sharing on their own time helps them learn how to be kind and giving. Forcing a child to share can create a feeling of resentment or loss. You may want to say, "When Andrea is done playing with the car, then you can have it."

## How to Teach Them Win-Win Negotiation

Have you ever yelled, "Stop fighting!"? Most of us have. But if you haven't taught children conflict resolution, it is highly unlikely they will stop. Teach children to negotiate a solution to their differences. A negotiation means that both kids get what they want and need. Negotiation is different from compromise, in which neither child is satisfied and they are both more concerned with what they gave up than what they acquired.

Here are some steps to resolving conflict:

1. Instead of bringing more fight to the fight, bring peace to the fight by calmly entering children's space and doing one of the following:

- Getting on their eye level
- Lovingly touching both of them
- Making friendly eye contact

2. If they are fighting over a toy, hold out your hand for the toy without saying anything or grabbing it. When it is placed in your hand, put the toy out of sight or behind your back.

3. Empathize with the most emotionally charged child first, and then the other.

4. Turn their attention away from the fight and switch their focus to what they want.

5. Ask them how they could work it out so they are both happy. Try using the phrase, "That's an idea!" to all their suggestions to avoid judging someone's idea as being better than another. Do not offer suggestions unless they get stuck.

6. Help them choose a solution.

7. Make sure they are both happy with the outcome.

8. Acknowledge them each specifically for skills they demonstrated. Begin the phrase with "I noticed" (e.g., "I noticed were patient," "I noticed you were creative," or "I noticed you stuck up for what you wanted."). This encourages them to identify helpful skills to resolve future conflict.

Children can't negotiate in the heat of anger. If they are angry, or become angry again, stop negotiating and go back to describing their differences and empathizing with them until they calm down.

Here is an example:

Jenny and Andrea are fighting over a shirt, and it's the kind of fight they have often. Mom has decided to do something different this time.

Jenny yells, "Give that shirt back to me!"

Andrea screams as she hits Jenny, "No, I had it first!"

Jenny hits back and yells, "Quit hitting me! You're ripping my shirt!"

Mom gets down on their level, strokes them lovingly on their backs, and observes, "It looks like you two are really angry with each other!"

Andrea, calming slightly, says: "Mom, Jenny took my shirt again without asking."

Mom says empathetically, "It's difficult to share clothes with one another."

Jenny replies, "Yeah, she won't let me wear her shirt."

Andrea retorts, "Well, you never ask me. You just take it and then you don't wash it. Then it's dirty when I want to wear it."

Mom empathizes again, "Jenny, you are frustrated because Andrea won't let you wear her shirt."

Mom then turns to Andrea and empathizes with her. "You want to be asked to wear the shirt, and you want it washed when she is done with it."

At this point, the girls are calm enough to pay attention when their mother starts to teach them conflict-resolution skills. Watch how careful she is to be nonjudgmental, to listen to both girls without taking sides, and to let them reach a solution themselves.

Mom asks, "Well, how could you both win?"

Jenny says, "She wants me to ask when I want to wear her shirt, and she wants me to wash it when I'm through."

Mom asks, "Is that accurate, Andrea?"

Andrea says, "Yeah, she never asks!"

Mom suggests, "So, if Jenny asks before she takes your shirt and she washes it when she's done, then you both will win?"

Andrea replies, "Yeah, that's right."

Mom says, "Andrea, I noticed that you stuck up for yourself and protected your belongings. Jenny, I notice that you were willing to respect your sister's wishes. It feels good to work things out."

The two girls have learned more by Mom doing a little coaching than if she had yelled at them or solved the problem herself.

You might be saying to yourself, "I don't have time to do this every time my children fight!" You don't have to. If you take the time to do these steps several times a week, they will soon be able to do it on their own.

Below are some other things you can do when your children fight:
- Leave the room.
- Do the unexpected, like join the fight in a playful manner.
- Ask them both to take a cooling-off period.
- If you are in a car, pull over to the side of the road and tell them *once*, "It is too dangerous for me to drive when there is fighting going on in my car." Wait silently until they quiet down and then start driving again.

Here is an example of how one mom handled her sons' fighting:

Mom was playing basketball with her two teenage sons. The boys were getting competitive, and soon they were pushing and shoving. The game was no longer fun for Mom. She said, "It's not fun for me when you two fight. When you're ready to make it fun again, come and get me. I'd love to play with you guys."

If you are a parent of a single child, these same principles work when a fight arises between friends or relatives. Children develop patterns of dealing with conflict that they will use for a lifetime. Some children learn to become victims, some bullies, and some learn healthy ways for handling conflict. The goal is not to stop or eliminate conflict but rather to teach your child how to deal with conflict effectively. Parents have an important role in which patterns their children will choose.

Parents often ignore or minimize fighting, hoping that it will stop or thinking that it's "simply child's play." It takes patience and courage for a parent to learn how to intervene effectively. It is best to take sibling rivalry seriously as children are learning skills now that they will use later as adults.

### Put Children in the Same Boat

*Crash!*

Mother rushed downstairs to find her favorite lamp shattered on the floor. "All right, who did this?" she demanded of her two children.

"Mike did it," squealed Sarah, pointing her finger accusingly at him.

"I did not, you liar. You did it," screamed Mike.

"You both know how I hate it when you lie. Now tell me, which one of you broke the lamp?" demanded Mother. Neither would fess up to the deed. Finally, Mother turned to Mike and said, "You always seem to get into trouble and you're the oldest. You should know better. Now clean up this mess!"

This mother has given her children negative attention and chosen sides rather than teaching them positive skills. She needs to go back upstairs and come down with a fresh viewpoint.

*Crash!*

Mother rushed downstairs to find her favorite lamp in pieces on the floor. She was extremely angry, so she stopped and took ten deep breaths until she calmed down. She said to the children, "It looks like you two had an accident."

Before she could say anything more, both kids began to accuse the other.

Mother put her arms around them and said, "I'm sad my lamp is broken. It doesn't matter who broke it. I wonder if you two would like some help cleaning up the pieces?" After the three of them cleaned up the mess, Mother said, "Would the two of you be willing to contribute fifty cents a week from now until Christmas to help pay for the lamp?"

"But, Mom, that's not fair! I didn't break it," wailed Sarah.

"Do you have a better idea?" Mother asked.

"Yeah, make Mike pay for it. He broke it," Sarah said.

Mother responded, "I'm not willing to do that. I don't want to take sides. If you have any other suggestions, let me know. In the meantime, I'll deduct fifty cents from both of your allowances."

You might be saying right now that the mother's action isn't fair. There is no way to be fair; there is a way to be effective. She didn't see who broke the lamp. She chose to put the children in the same boat and hold them both accountable for the accident. Neither child was made to feel special, either for being good or being bad. The child who is the troublemaker often changes his or her behavior when he or she no longer gets special attention for it. No one's tattling was acknowledged. In addition, the mother modeled handling anger in a healthy way.

Here is another option if your children are fighting over a toy and you have already taught them how to negotiate: Hold out your hand for the object that they're fighting over. After they give you the object, tell them, "You may have the toy back when the two of you come to agreement about it. I'll be in the study." Then leave the room with the toy and let them work out their problem. Don't use intimidation to get them to stop fighting. Avoid saying, "You're driving me crazy with your fighting!" or, "If you don't stop fighting, I'm going to put you in your rooms!"

## Handling Fighting While Driving

I was driving the camp van when two campers began to argue. I didn't say a word but looked for a safe place to pull the van over. I stopped, took the keys, got out, and sat down on the hillside. One of the kids came to me and asked, "What's wrong?"

I said, "It's not safe for me to drive when there is arguing, so I'm waiting until you're finished."

The boy ran back to the van and reported to the others. Soon the boys called out, "Come on back. We solved the argument."

I got back in the van, and we continued. On the way back to camp, another argument erupted. As soon as I began to slow down, the boys stopped fighting.

Sometimes it is neither safe nor convenient to stop the car when children fight. In that case, you may have to do something different. One dad told his children that he would turn around and go home if they didn't stop arguing by the time he reached the stoplight. They didn't stop, so he kept his word and turned around. If you want kids to learn, follow through instead of making idle threats.

## Stay Out of the Fight

Sometimes a parent's best response to a fight is to stay out of it. This is particularly true if the children are fighting to get your attention. You will need to teach them how to get your attention more appropriately, but for now you want to remove yourself from their vicinity so that they will quit fighting.

If you're worried that the children might damage something in the house, firmly and gently guide them outside. If you think they might hurt each other, remain silently vigilant in an out-of-the-way spot.

Leave the area or the house altogether if the kids are old enough. Don't say anything as you go.

> My sister and I used to fight when we were children. Our parents tried lots of ideas to get us to stop, including putting us in the corner or making us kiss ("Yuck!") and make up. Even though we were forced to stop fighting, we were still angry with each other. One day during a fight, my mother left the house without saying a word. When we realized she was gone, we recognized how much our fighting both-ered her. We quit fighting, and we cleaned up the kitchen to make her feel better.

Mother's departure made more of an impact on us than punishment ever did. She left the choice to stop fighting up to us. While she was gone, we worked together as a team, and that brought us closer.

## Act in an Unexpected Way

Try dispelling tension or a fight by doing something unexpected. For exam-ple, if your children are calling each other names, join in playfully. If they are starting to roughhouse too angrily, propose a walk or a game of ball together.

> Josh angrily yelled at Andrea, "You're a stupid cow!"
> Andrea yelled back, "Well, you're a stupid monkey's breath."
> Dad heard this exchange and after observing for a few seconds, said lightly, "This is a great game," and turned to Josh, "You're a

slimy, green piece of mildewed spaghetti left over in the refrigerator!"
They all laughed, and that dissipated the fight.

## Tattling or Telling

Children tattle to get others in trouble, to get attention, or to get you to solve their problem. If you tell them to solve their problem themselves, or teach them to get attention appropriately, they will usually quit tattling. If your child says, "Mom, Jared hit me!" say, "That must hurt. I wonder how you'll handle that?"

Teach them the distinction between tattling and telling. Tattling is usually trying to get the other child in trouble. On the other hand, telling is informing an adult when someone is in trouble and needs help or a child is being a bully and intervention is necessary.

## Address Jealousy and Anger

It seems impossible to keep children from feeling jealous of one another because we can never control how they're going to interpret what they hear and see. However, you can correct them when they think you favor one of them over the other, and you can minimize the discomfort of jealousy. Teach your children that they are whole and complete in themselves without being the same as their sibling.

> Jennifer complained to Mom, "I'm not as smart as Nathan."
>
> Mom said, "It's not important that you be the same. I love the fact that you're different from Nathan. Both of you are smart in your own, unique ways. Why would I want two Nathans? Besides, if you decide you want to get good grades, you'll be amazed at what you can do."

Be careful not to compare a child to his or her sibling; be careful that you do not favor one child over another. Parents who try to make everything fair for each child are fighting a losing battle and giving both children the wrong message that life should be fair. Children whose parents honor and nurture their individual differences feel less competitive toward other children, even if they are jealous at times.

## Understanding Sibling Competition

Sibling competition does not necessarily mean one child beats up on the other. Another way to compete is for one child to avoid comparison by giving up in an area where his or her sibling succeeds. One child might excel in music and the other in sports. Often, the child who doesn't do well in the area of his or her sibling's expertise feels that he or she doesn't have talent in that area. In reality, this child has only given up. With practice, this child, too, could achieve in that area, if he or she chooses.

Children can compete in other subtle ways. You may have a "good" child and a "bad" child. Listen to this woman's admission:

> I must confess that in my family, I was the "good" girl, and I had a brother who was always getting punished. One day, we were behind the garage, where there was a sledgehammer. I looked at my brother and said, "Boy, that sure looks heavy, doesn't it?"
>
> He said, "Yeah, it sure does."
>
> I said tauntingly, "I bet it would really hurt if someone got hit with it." He got a big grin on his face and leaned over to pick up the hammer. I said, "If you hit me with that, I'm telling!"
>
> He picked it up and tapped me on the shoulder.
>
> I ran into the house screaming, "Mommy, Andy hit me with a sledgehammer!" Mother held me until I quieted down, and then she lectured and spanked Andy. I felt pretty smug about the whole thing.

You can see that sometimes the younger sibling is not the poor innocent victim he or she pretends to be. If you have a "good" child and a "bad" child and you decide to work on the "bad" child's behavior, be prepared for some surprises. When your parenting becomes effective at changing the "bad" child's behavior, your "good" child may start to misbehave. Believe it or not, this is a sign of progress. Pat yourself on the back because it means you have succeeded in making the behavior of both children inappropriate. You have disturbed the equilibrium.

# 15

# Putting It All Together

These are the steps to redirecting children's behavior that you have learned in reading this book. The steps here are in brief form to help you remember the new philosophy and the skills that enable you to redirect children effectively.

**1. Establish and maintain a relationship of acceptance and mutual respect with your child.** Make a loving connection with eye contact, touch, and an accepting tone of voice. Encourage your child to express his or her own opinions and feelings.

**2. Gain insight into your child's mistaken goal.** You can determine his or her goal by the way the child's behavior makes you feel.

**3. Help your child identify his or her mistaken goal** in a nonaccusing way. Children are often unaware of what they're doing. This step brings the goal into the child's consciousness and gives him or her the opportunity to make a different choice.

Speak in nonjudgmental terms:

- For the goal of attention say, "It feels like you need some attention. How else could you get my attention?" instead of "Stop being so annoying."
- For the goal of power say, "This feels like a power struggle. I love you too much to fight with you!" instead of "You are being so stubborn."

- For the goal of revenge say, "That hurts. Did I do something to hurt you?" instead of "I can't believe you just said that. You are so ungrateful!"
- For the goal of avoidance say, "This feels very frustrating, and you would rather avoid doing it?" instead of, "Quit being a baby and just do it!"

It is vital that your intention be one of understanding and curiosity, and that it will cause your child to self-reflect. If you are unable, for whatever reason, to speak in a nonaccusing way, skip step 3 because you will only make matters worse.

**4. Arrange or allow a situation that makes your child's goal inappropriate.** Methods that you can use to make a child's behavior inappropriate are in the goal identification and redirection sections in this book.

**5. Redirect behavior** by providing opportunities for your children to:

- Express needs and wants without acting inappropriately.
- Handle hurts without hurting back.
- Be powerful in appropriate ways.
- Be helpful and recognize the value of feeling worthwhile.
- Be cooperative and recognize how much more can be achieved by working as a team.
- Be gentle with themselves and allow themselves to make mistakes.
- Do what they can to make the situation more enjoyable.
- Learn that problems don't need to be "fixed," but only improved.

This last step is crucial because if you just stop their misbehavior, children will find another avenue to misbehave since you have worked only on the symptom and not the cause of the behavior. Step 5 provides a healthier way to channel their inappropriate energy.

## Our Children, Our Future

The way we parent will, to a large extent, determine the future of our society. We have a choice: to parent in a way that teaches our children to be uncooperative, self-serving, irresponsible, and disconnected, or to raise children who hold values intentionally, are compassionate, and maintain and nurture close relationships. The choice is ours.

I do not intend to make you feel guilty—as we know, guilt serves no one. My intention, instead, is to increase your awareness of how your actions affect our entire society. I strongly urge you to become more conscious. Don't settle for less than you can do! Set goals for the way you want your family to function, and then consciously create the family of your heart's deepest desire. You and your family are extremely capable and creative. The fact that you are reading this book tells me of your concern, and I applaud and appreciate your commitment.

It is no easy task to change old patterns. Make sure you are gentle with yourself. Find someone to support you—perhaps a partner, a friend, or a parenting class. Without support, it's all too easy to slip back into old, ineffective ways.

Most important of all, love one another and be good to one another. The individual members of your family can function like a battery—that is, a collective recharging source of encouragement and support that allows all of you to go out into the community and contribute to it. There is nothing more important than loving someone and being loved. Remember this: lean into love.

## A Child's Request

Dear Mommy and Daddy,

Hold me, touch me, snuggle me often, for it is through your love that I flourish.

Watch me, listen to me, take your time with me when you read *Green Eggs and Ham* to me at night, for I judge my importance by how important I am to you.

Be patient, understand me first, whenever possible help me to get what I want, for it is through your interactions with me that I learn to interact with others.

Don't be afraid to be firm with me, for it is through your firmness that I learn the courage to care. Don't bribe me, reward me, or punish me, for you rob me of the opportunity to listen to my own internal voice. Don't hit me or yell at me, for this teaches me to use force to get my way.

Forgive yourself quickly, for my spirit is resilient.

Instead of remembering my footprints on your windshield, my impish protests, and the hole I put in the wall, remember the day I discovered my shadow, my arms around your neck, and the delight of my giggles.

I will remember your butterfly kisses, your open arms, dancing in the rain with you, and the plastic frog you put under my eggs at breakfast more than the toys and clothes you bought for me.

On our bad days, watch me while I sleep. Marvel at my eyelashes, cheekbones, and fingertips, and remind yourself of how much you love me.

When given a choice, assume the best of me and expect the best for me.

Stand by me, but let me fight my own battles, for it is here that I develop my own strength and build my own character.

Support my ever-changing dreams. I need someone to believe in me when I don't.

Trust me as a teen, even though there is no evidence that you should. Trust that you have taught me well.

Allow me to express who I am and make my life's decisions, even though they differ from yours.

Last, make nothing other than God more important than our family, for it is here that I discover who I am.

—*Kathryn J. Kvols*

# Acknowledgments

**First and foremost,** I would like to thank my family: my husband, Brian, for endless support, love, and gentle nudging; my son, Tyler, who taught me what unconditional love means; Brianna, who helps me remember to be silly; Chloe, Amy, Emily, and Cindy Harper, who are teaching me what it means to be a blended family.

Thank you also to my former husband Bill Riedler, who coauthored the first edition of this book. I especially appreciate the great father he was to our son, Tyler.

A very special thank-you goes to all the instructors of the Redirecting Children's Behavior course, who have encouraged and supported me for many years. Bob Hoekstra, Dr. Tim and Ann Jordan, RN, Helen Hall, APN, Lucinda Hudgins, Lesley Iwinkski, MD, Lisa Lakner, and Carol Watson are but a few who inspired me in this work. Betty Towry, PhD, has been a great friend, as well as my confidante.

I acknowledge the late Rudolf Dreikurs, MD, for being the main source of inspiration for *Redirecting Children's Behavior.*

# Appendix

# Common Behaviors:
# Ages Eighteen Months
# to Eighteen Years

What follows is a brief summary of the normal behaviors of children at different ages. When you understand why your children are doing what they're doing, it's easier to muster the patience to deal with the behavior. Also, many parents worry if their children are normal. Biting and hitting are behaviors of concern to parents of two-year-olds. This behavior is quite normal for a toddler. Knowing this fact lets a parent breathe a sigh of relief. However, just because the behavior is normal at this stage does not mean that it goes undisciplined.

The Gesell Institute for Human Development suggest that easy ages tend to alternate with difficult ages. Ages of equilibrium (inward looking, quiet, withdrawn) tend to be followed by ages of disequilibrium (outward looking, exuberant, expansive). Easier times are followed by more difficult times. A breakup of a calmer period usually is followed by a more mature stage of development.

Don't get concerned if your child is ahead or behind these stages, or if the descriptions don't even resemble what your child does. Every child is an individual. One child may exhibit some of these behaviors while a sibling from the same family may not.

There are many delightful qualities during each age that far outweigh the negatives, or challenges, that you see here. However, this book concentrates on how to redirect misbehavior, so the information here is particularly helpful in that regard.

Read the stage before and after your child's age for more information that may be relevant to your situation.

## *Normal, yet Possibly Annoying, Behaviors*

### *Eighteen Months*

Is negative, says "no" often

Does the opposite of what is requested

Does not want to share; everything is "my" or "mine"

Often hits, kicks, and bites

Lacks patience, wants it now

Tests limits (can be quite exhausting)

May climb out of crib

Refuses to eat certain foods

Regresses to baby food or bottle

Clings anxiously or walks away from parent

Hates to see doors closed

May be afraid of strangers, including grandparents

Notices and overreacts to small differences

Resists diaper change

Sucks thumb; requires "blankie"

Fears tubs and baths

Explores genitalia

Tries to walk away from parent whenever possible

Does not play with other children; plays alongside them or alone

Does not sit very long for cuddling; stiffens and slides off lap

### *Two Years Old*

Has difficulty making decisions; changes mind even when you know
    the child wants what is being offered

Throws temper tantrums, which can be violent

Demands that things remain the same

May favor one parent over the other

Is bossy and demanding

May start to stutter

Thumb-sucking may intensify

Dawdles

Shifts quickly from being capable ("Me do it") to incapable ("Mommy do it")

Is easily frustrated

Does not like to be physically restricted

Is not interested in pleasing you

*Three Years Old*

Hands may tremble

Is confused about which hand to use

Stutters

May complain about problems with vision

Seems like nothing pleases him or her

Makes commands like "Don't look at me," "Don't talk"

Is emotionally inconsistent: one minute shy, next minute too bold

Indulges in nail-biting, thumb-sucking, nose-picking, and rubbing his or her genitals

Expresses fears

May be cooperative with a babysitter and a monster with you

May quit napping

May still wet the bed

*Four Years Old*

Talks too much

Incessantly asks, "Why?"

Is fascinated with bowel movements

Uses words related to elimination, like "poopoo head"

Swears and cusses

Demands can be annoyingly persistent

Excludes certain children from play

Wants to know exact details on difficult subjects

*Five Years Old*

Tends to be brash, combative, indecisive, overdemanding, and explosive

Becomes more challenging in rebellion: "Try and make me!" is a typical stance

Once an emotional outburst has started, may have a hard time stopping it

Has difficulty grasping a pencil and may change grasps frequently

Talks too much

Has difficulty admitting that he or she has done anything wrong

May take things that don't belong to him or her

Talks with mouth full

Can dress self, but frequently refuses or says, "I can't"

May still suck thumb, pick nose, bite nails

May clear throat frequently and make clicking or smacking noises

May be fascinated by fire; may want to start fires

*Six Years Old*

Is extremely ambivalent; can't make up mind

Reverses numbers and letters

Wants to be the first, the best, the winner

Failure is unbearable

Has difficulty accepting criticism

Is loud and demanding

Acts "fresh"

Is very sensitive emotionally

Doesn't always tell the truth

Frequently steals

Has bad table manners

May have an occasional toileting accident

May refuse to bathe

Engages in battles about dressing

Doesn't take care of clothes

Scalp is very tender and sensitive

Makes irritating throaty noises

Is clumsy
Complains of aches and pains

*Seven Years Old*
May be afraid that others don't like him or her
Worries
Minor illness may be magnified to fatality status
Accuses parents of liking other siblings more
Is easily disappointed
Has a tendency to do one thing for too long
Is too anxious to be perfect
Complains about how others treat him or her (teachers, siblings, friends)
Has many fears
Is easily distracted at mealtime

*Eight Years Old*
Does everything fast
Feels extremely sensitive to perceived criticism from others
Experiences self-doubt
Hard on him- or herself for making mistakes
Exaggerates problems and dilemmas
Wants a lot of communication with primary caretaker. Frequently asks,
   "What?"
Highly aware of others' mistakes and points them out
Is not a good self-starter
Loves to argue
Wants to wear "what other kids are wearing"
Is accident prone
May refuse to take baths
Has strong interest in possessions, may hoard or gloat over them

*Nine Years Old*
May now seem to resent parents' presence
Wants more freedom

Wants a lot of social activity

Has mood swings

Worries and complains

Is so busy with own activity that seems unaware of others

Wants fairness

Bathing can still be a problem

Lays considerable blame and emphasis on who started what

*Ten Years Old*

Anger is often violent

Plots revenge

Has being the butt of a joke

Asks personal questions

May express concern if isn't developing physically like others

A girl will hunch her shoulders if she's uncomfortable about breast
    development

*Eleven Years Old*

Makes no effort to cooperate

Is quick to criticize

Expects perfection from others, challenges rules and restrictions

Loves to argue

Is physically violent; may hit, kick, or slam doors

Yells, swears, talks back, says mean and sarcastic things

Likes to gossip

Has intense need to be right or to know it all

Makes references to your "old age"

Needs sleep

Has difficulty with siblings close in age

Wants radio or television on while doing homework

Is always on the phone

May cheat

May steal with peers

Has mood swings

*Twelve Years Old*

Doing things on weekends with friends is crucial; if he or she can't, he or she may become sullen and depressed

Expresses boredom if friends are unavailable

May not want you to purchase clothes for him or her anymore

May walk ahead of you or behind you

May not want to be touched in public

*Thirteen Years Old*

Is uncommunicative

Withdraws to room frequently

Demands more privacy and accuses you of prying

Is uncertain about self and life in general

May be unfriendly and unhappy

Worries about body features

Does not want to be understood

Has fewer friends

Speaks in a low voice

Shrugs his or her shoulders

Feels teachers are unjust

May be found crying in his or her room

Worries about everything

Expressions of affection don't come easily

Doesn't often confide in parents

Is embarrassed by parents

*Fourteen Years Old*

In public, wants to be as far away from you as possible

Picks at the way you dress or look

Revolts against your old-fashioned ways

Picks apart social systems: school, organized religion, law enforcement, etc.

May challenge cherished family values

*Fifteen Years Old*
Wants to be totally independent and free
Angry at parents who don't see him or her as ready for independence
Age where the family is most unsatisfactory
Friends mean the most
Has difficulty getting along with the same-sex parent
Does things that cause you great anxiety
Withdraws emotional contact with parent

*Sixteen to Eighteen Years Old*
Experience considerable anxiety about wanting to leave home and they
    doubt their ability to succeed
Feel anxious about what they're going to choose for a career
Considerable confusion about their future
Often engage in risky behaviors

# Other Helpful Parenting Books

Ames, Louise Bates, and Carol Chase Haber. *Your One-Year-Old*. New York: Dell, 1989. (Series continues with books covering each age up to fourteen years.)

Beattie, Melody. *The Language of Letting Go*. New York: HarperCollins, 1990.

Bloomfield, Harold. *Making Peace in Your Stepfamily*. New York: Hyperion, 1993.

Bluestein, Jane. *The Parent's Little Book of Lists: Dos and Don'ts of Effective Parenting*. Deerfield Beach, FL: Health Communications, 1997.

Briggs, Dorothy Corkille. *Your Child's Self Esteem*. New York: Doubleday, 1970.

Clarke-Fields, Hunter. *Raising Good Human Beings*. Oakland, CA: New Harbinger, 2019.

Crary, Elizabeth. *Help! The Kids Are at It Again: Using Kids' Quarrels to Teach "People" Skills*. Chicago: Parenting Press, 1997.

Dreikurs, Rudolf. *Children: The Challenge*. New York: Penguin USA, 1991.

Dreikurs, Rudolf, Bernice Bronia Grunwald, and Floy C. Pepper. *Maintaining Sanity in the Classroom: Classroom Management Techniques*. New York: HarperCollins, 1982.

Dweck, Carol. *Mindset*. New York: Ballantine Books, 2006.

Faber, Adele, and Elaine Mazlich. *How to Talk So Kids Will Listen & Listen So Kids Will Talk*. New York: Avon Books, 1980.

Ford, Judy. *Wonderful Ways to Love a Child*. Berkeley: Conari Press, 1996.

Gerwirtz, Abigail. *When the World Feels Like a Scary Place*. Workman, 2020.

Glenn, H. Stephen, and Jane Nelsen. *Raising Self-Reliant Children in a Self-Indulgent World*. Rocklin, CA: Prima Publishing, 1989.

Greene, Ross W. *The Explosive Child*. New York: HarperCollins, 1998 Quill, 2001.

Kohn, Alfie. *Punished by Rewards*. Boston: Houghton Mifflin, 1993.

Kurcinka, Mary Sheedy. *Raising Your Spirited Child*. New York: Harper Perennial, 1992.

McCourt, Lisa. *Juicy Joy*. Carlsbad, CA: Hay House, 2012.

Miller, Jennifer. *Confident Parents, Confident Kids: Raising Emotional Intelligence in Ourselves and Our Kids—from Toddlers to Teenagers*. Beverly, MA: Fair Wind Press, 2020.

Natterson, Cara. *Decoding Boys: New Science Behind the Subtle Art of Raising Sons*. New York: Ballantine Books, 2020

Nelsen, Jane, and Lynn Lott. *I'm on Your Side*. Rocklin, CA: Prima Publishing, 1990.

Neville, Helen, and Diane Clark Johnson. *Temperament Tools: Working with Your Child's Inborn Traits*. Chicago, Parenting Press, 1998.

Pipher, Mary. *Reviving Ophelia: Saving the Selves of Adolescent Girls*. New York: Ballantine Books, 1995.

———. *The Shelter of Each Other*. New York: Riverhead Books, 2008.

Siegel, Daniel, and Tina Payne Bryson. *The Power of Showing Up: How Parental Presence Shapes Who Our Kids Become and How Their Brains Get Wired*. New York: Ballantine Books, 2020.

———. *The Whole-Brain Child*. New York: Delacorte, 2011.

Sunderland, Margot. *The Science of Parenting*. New York: DK, 2006.

West, Kim. *The Sleep Lady's Good Night, Sleep Tight*. New York: Hachette, 2020.

# Index

*Note: Entries in italics refer to charts*

# About the Author

**K**athryn J. Kvols is president of the Academy for Parenting Education and Coaching, a company she started thirty years ago (under a different name at that time) to educate parents in the methods of peaceful parenting. Her life has been richly filled as a mental health counselor, a facilitator of personal growth workshops, and a director of a summer camp for children.

Kathryn struggled with her parenting skills. Being brought up with a strict, shame-based discipline, Kathryn knew she wanted something different for her children and her own peace of mind.

During her thirty years of study on best parenting practices, she wrote the book *Redirecting Children's Behavior* and its companion parenting course. This course is being taught in twenty-one countries and has been translated into five languages. Her researched-based strategies have empowered thousands of parents to redirect their kids' *mis*behaviors into positive outcomes without nagging, yelling, or taking away privileges.

Her latest work is Whining, Tears, and Tantrums Oh My!, a course for parents and caregivers for children sixteen months to six years old.

Kathryn is a sought-after international speaker, writer, trainer, and parenting coach who believes her most important role has been as mother to her children. Her experiences as a mom of five, a single mom, and stepmom make her a compassionate and effective facilitator. From every course and speech she presents, her participants walk away with practical tools they can implement immediately.

### Redirecting Children's Behavior Parenting Course

*Your next step:* Take a life-changing Redirecting Children's Behavior Course near you. The Academy for Parenting Education and Coaching provides parenting courses and other materials helpful to you in your parenting journey. Call for information on courses near you, or visit https://www.apecparenting.com to find out how you can become a parent education instructor.